Lesson Study

This book introduces Lesson Study (LS) in the UK, making its origins as a Lesson Study in Japan, East Asia, Americas and Europe. It explores impact LS in schools and educational institutions, providing examples of compelling, externally evaluated impact outcomes for both primary learners and teacher learners, and vivid exemplars of LS in action across age ranges and curricular contexts.

Each chapter presents international research outcomes that clearly demonstrate how and why LS has a place within teacher learning approaches that have the greatest impact and the greatest capacity building potential for creating outstanding teaching. This is supported by primary research evidence, and linked with contemporary and recent high quality research worldwide into pupil learning, teacher learning, school improvement and system improvement. The book illustrates the diverse application of LS for innovating or transferring highly effective practices in a variety of contexts to boost learning for children with a range of challenges and specific needs.

Lesson Study provides a global perspective on the development of LS worldwide, exploring its impact on innovation, creativity, curricula and achievement in a variety of contexts. It will be of key interest to practitioners in schools and teacher education institutions, researchers, and policy and decision makers at local, national and international levels. The book's explicit focus on the leadership of local authorities will also make it valuable reading for all leaders of professional development and school improvement.

Peter Dudley is an education leader in Camden, visiting Professor of Education at Leicester University, Secretary of the World Association of Lesson Studies and founder of Lesson Study UK.

Routledge Research in Education

For a complete list of titles in this series, please visit www.routledge.com

95 The Resegregation of Schools
Education and race in the twenty-
first century
*Edited by Jamel K. Donnor and
Adrienne D. Dixson*

**96 Autobiographical Writing and
Identity in EFL Education**
Shizhou Yang

**97 Online Learning and
Community Cohesion**
Linking schools
Roger Austin and Bill Hunter

**98 Language Teachers and
Teaching**
Global perspectives, local initiatives
*Edited by Selim Ben Said and
Lawrence Jun Zhang*

**99 Towards Methodologically
Inclusive Research Syntheses**
Expanding possibilities
Harsh Suri

**100 Raising Literacy Achievement
in High-Poverty Schools**
An evidence-based approach
Eithne Kennedy

**101 Learning and Collective
Creativity**
Activity-theoretical and sociocultural
studies
Annalisa Sannino and Viv Ellis

102 Educational Inequalities
Difference and diversity in schools
and higher education
*Edited by Kalwant Bhopal and
Uvanney Maylor*

**103 Education, Social Background
and Cognitive Ability**
The decline of the social
Gary N. Marks

**104 Education in Computer
Generated Environments**
Sara de Freitas

**105 The Social Construction of
Meaning**
Reading literature in urban English
classrooms
John Yandell

**106 Global Perspectives on
Spirituality in Education**
*Edited by Jacqueline Watson, Marian
de Souza and Ann Trousdale*

107 Neo-liberal Educational Reforms
A critical analysis
*Edited by David A. Turner and
Hüseyin Yolcu*

**108 The Politics of Pleasure in
Sexuality Education**
Pleasure bound
*Edited by Louisa Allen, Mary Lou
Rasmussen, and Kathleen Quinlivan*

109 **Popular Culture, Pedagogy and Teacher Education**
International perspectives
Edited by Phil Benson and Alice Chik

110 **Teacher Training and the Education of Black Children**
Bringing color into difference
Uvanney Maylor

111 **Secrecy and Tradecraft in Educational Administration**
The covert side of educational life
Eugenie A. Samier

112 **Affirming Language Diversity in Schools and Society**
Beyond linguistic apartheid
Edited by Pierre Wilbert Orelus

113 **Teacher Leadership**
New conceptions for autonomous student learning in the age of the Internet
Kokila Roy Katyal and Colin Evers

114 **Test Fraud**
Statistical detection and methodology
Edited by Neal M. Kingston and Amy K. Clark

115 **Literacy, Play and Globalization**
Converging imaginaries in children's critical and cultural performances
Carmen Liliana Medina and Karen E. Wohlwend

116 **Biotechnology, Education and Life Politics**
Debating genetic futures from school to society
Pádraig Murphy

117 **Vernaculars in the Classroom**
Paradoxes, pedagogy, possibilities
Shondel Nero and Dohra Ahmad

118 **Professional Uncertainty, Knowledge and Relationship in the Classroom**
A psycho-social perspective
Joseph Mintz

119 **Negotiating Privilege and Identity in Educational Contexts**
Adam Howard, Aimee Polimeno, and Brianne Wheeler

120 **Liberty and Education**
A civic republican approach
Geoffrey Hinchliffe

121 **Constructing Narratives of Continuity and Change**
A transdisciplinary approach to researching lives
Edited by Hazel Reid and Linden West

122 **Education, Philosophy and Wellbeing**
New perspectives on the work of John White
Edited by Judith Suissa, Carrie Winstanley and Roger Marples

123 **Chinese Students' Writing in English**
Implications from a corpus-driven study
Maria Leedham

124 **9/11 and Collective Memory in US Classrooms**
Teaching about Terror
Cheryl Lynn Duckworth

125 **African Americans and Homeschooling**
Motivations, opportunities and challenges
Ama Mazama and Garvey Musumunu

126 **Lesson Study**
Professional learning for our time
Edited by Peter Dudley

Lesson Study

Professional learning for our time

Edited by Peter Dudley

Routledge
Taylor & Francis Group

LONDON AND NEW YORK

First published 2015
by Routledge
2 Park Square, Milton Park, Abingdon, Oxfordshire OX14 4RN

and by Routledge
711 Third Avenue, New York, NY 10017

First issued in paperback 2016

Routledge is an imprint of the Taylor & Francis Group, an informa business

© 2015 P. Dudley

British Library Cataloguing in Publication Data
A catalogue record for this book is available from the British Library

Library of Congress Cataloging-in-Publication Data
Lesson study : professional learning for our time / edited by Peter Dudley.
1. Special education–Great Britain. 2. Lesson planning–Great Britain.
I. Dudley, Peter, 1957 March 13-
LC3986.G7L47 2014
371.90941–dc23
2014014148

ISBN 13: 978-1-138-21862-8 (pbk)
ISBN 13: 978-0-415-70265-2 (hbk)

Typeset in Times
by Cenveo Publisher Services

For my mother whose daily stories of her pupils' struggles and successes helped me to understand from a young age that every learner learns differently.

Contents

About the contributors   xi
Foreword: Lesson Study as a strategic choice for CPD   xv
CHARLES DESFORGES

Acknowledgements   xxi

1   How Lesson Study works and why it creates excellent
    learning and teaching   1
    PETER DUDLEY

2   Lesson Study: an international review of the research   29
    HAIYAN XU AND DAVID PEDDER

3   Leading Lesson Study in schools and across school systems   59
    JIM O'SHEA, SUE TEAGUE, GILL JORDAN, JEAN LANG
    AND PETER DUDLEY

4   How Lesson Study helps teachers of pupils with specific
    needs or difficulties   86
    ANNAMARI YLONEN AND BRAHM NORWICH

5   Lesson Study in initial teacher education   107
    WASYL CAJKLER AND PHIL WOOD

6   Evolving the curriculum through Lesson Study in Japan   128
    HIROYUKI KUNO

7   Prospects for further development of Lesson Study   145
    DAVID PEDDER

Index   152

About the contributors

Wasyl Cajkler is Senior Lecturer in Education at the University of Leicester. His research interests focus on Lesson Study (LS) in teacher education, second and foreign language learning and pedagogy. He has written on the preparation of teachers for diversity in the classroom, teacher learning and grammar in the curriculum, and LS. Currently, he is chair of the Lesson Study Research Group at the School of Education, University of Leicester.

Charles Desforges is Emeritus Professor at the University of Exeter. He now works as an independent researcher and educational consultant with special interests in teaching, learning, parental involvement and school leadership. He has been a research adviser to a number of government bodies in the UK and overseas. His current work involves supporting the professional development of head teachers and teachers. From 1998 to 2002 he was the Director of the Teaching and Learning Research Programme of the Economic and Social Research Council, the largest coordinated programme of social research ever undertaken in the UK. Professor Desforges was awarded an OBE in the 2004 New Years Honours list for Services to Education.

Peter Dudley is Assistant Director for Educational Achievement at the London Borough of Camden and Visiting Professor of Education at the University of Leicester. He introduced LS to the UK in 2001. He has since developed LS across the UK in his former role as Director of the Primary National Strategy and internationally in his role as the Secretary of the World Association of Lesson Study (WALS) based in Singapore. His study of 'How Teachers Learn in contexts of Lesson Study' was runner up in the British Educational Research Association's Doctoral Research Awards in 2012. Pete is the founder and owner of www.lessonstudy.co.uk

Gill Jordan is a literacy specialist and a well known exponent of LS. She has conducted her own lesson studies and supported teachers and schools leaders to do so in both primary and secondary schools. She has written about LS and presented her lesson studies internationally. She is a member of the World Association of Lesson Study (WALS) and is currently an expert adviser to a large national research programme investigating the effectiveness of LS for raising standards.

Hiroyuki Kuno Associate Professor of Education at Nagoya University, is an expert in Lesson Study and School Development. He has been actively leading LS activities in schools across Japan and internationally in countries such as Singapore, and Indonesia. His research interests include LS, Lesson Analysis and Integrated-Studies. In his social responsibilities at a national level in Japan, he serves as an editorial member of the National Curriculum Integrated Studies committee at the Ministry of Education. Dr Kuno is a founder and executive committee member of the WALS Council. He was a visiting scholar at University of Cambridge in 2013.

Jean Lang Following extensive experience as an Early Years and Primary teacher and headteacher, Jean has provided support to schools and national and local government for the past 15 years. She introduced LS into schools which required improvement in a large Shire County increasing performance significantly and then replicated this work nationally across England. For the past three years she has been Head of Primary School Improvement in Camden and has introduced LS to teachers and practitioners working with children and students from the ages of 0 to 13. Jean presented her Camden work at the WALS conference in Gothenburg, 2013 and is a WALS Council member.

Brahm Norwich is Professor of Educational Psychology and Special Educational Needs at the Graduate School of Education, University of Exeter. He was principal investigator of a three-year project about using LS to improve the teaching and learning of pupils with learning difficulties. The project produced programmes and materials including a book: Norwich, B. and Jones, J. (eds) (2014) *Lesson Study: Making a Difference to Teaching Pupils with Learning Difficulties*, London: Bloomsbury. The project also led to the development of LS as an assessment strategy to investigate learning difficulties based on a response to teaching model.

Jim O'Shea is Headteacher at St Aloysius Catholic Junior School in Camden, London. LS has been an integral part of joint practice development at his school since 2010. Jim has played a leading role in helping to establish LS across Camden schools and beyond.

David Pedder is Professor of Education, Director of Research at the University of Leicester School of Education and a member of the University of Leicester's Lesson Study Group. His research interests are concerned with the processes, practices, perspectives and conditions that support improvement in teaching and learning in classrooms. He is working closely in partnership with a network of schools (Teaching School Alliances in the East Midlands area of England) to promote LS as a way of supporting in the production, mobilisation and use of research by school teachers and leaders at scale.

Sue Teague is the Headteacher of Caddington Village School, which provides education for over 500 children aged 3 to 13. The school was formed in 2008 following the merger of three schools. Sue introduced LS after leading the school's involvement in a research project initiated by the University of Exeter. LS was used to build a community of practice and provide high quality, relevant staff development; it has been embraced by the whole school and driven school improvement from within. Sue is passionate about education and believes that teachers have the ability to unlock learning for children in their care.

Phil Wood is a Senior Lecturer in the School of Education, University of Leicester. He has interests in researching teaching and learning innovations from which his interest in LS has grown. As a member of the Lesson Study Research Group in the School of Education he has played a part in developing projects in a number of local schools as well as applying the process at both Initial Teacher Education and Higher Education levels. He is also currently beginning to explore how LS can be located in wider educational debates.

Haiyan Xu is currently a PhD candidate at the University of Leicester. Her research interest in LS developed from her personal and professional experiences as an English language teacher, a role within which she not only practised LS as a routine part of her professional development but was also invited many times to conduct public lessons in open house LS events held at municipal and national levels in China. Her PhD research focuses on the processes through which LS supports teacher professional learning and practice development attuned to the latest round of curriculum reform in China.

Annamari Ylonen is a Research Associate at University of Cambridge, UK and lead evaluator in the Camden New Curriculum Mathematics Lesson Study Program. Previously, she worked as a Research Fellow at the University of Exeter, UK. She has been involved in LS research in the UK and abroad since 2009. She has recently led a LS school improvement project in Qatar and continues to publish in this area. Annamari's research interests include social justice, market-oriented education reforms in Finland and globally, and teacher professional development.

Foreword

Lesson Study as a strategic choice for CPD

Charles Desforges

The most direct route to improved standards in education is taken to be through improving the quality of teaching in classrooms. In recognition of this, significant investment has been made in teacher continuing professional development (CPD) over recent decades. Sadly it is hard to find evidence of the impact of this investment on student outcomes. Classically teacher CPD has taken the form of events outside of the classroom. It has been assumed that teachers transform this experience into enhanced classroom practice. This approach to CPD has been under-researched in the sense that evidence has not, in the main, been collected on the impact of such work on student learning progress. Where such evidence has been collected it has proven extremely diffi-cult to draw persuasive conclusions about what works, what works best and for whom (Opfer and Pedder, 2011). Notwithstanding this conclu-sion, some reviewers have argued that it is possible to discern in the CPD research some broad principles to guide those who design and manage CPD (Timperley, 2008; Desimone, 2011).

Lesson Study (LS) with its very long history is, to a significant degree, immune to these conclusions. This is because LS takes place in classrooms with the expressed purpose of enhancing student learning directly. There is no 'transfer of training' issue. That said, the evalua-tion of LS as a strategic choice for CPD is only now being undertaken to the rigorous standards of contemporary researchers. This research should identify the scale of the impact and its sustainability. The best and latest of this work is reported in this volume. In advance of defini-tive outcomes of this research this book aims to show how powerful and attractive LS is. It will comment on the authenticity of LS in regard to real classrooms, the consistency of LS procedures with respect to current theories of learning and the alignment of LS approaches with the criteria for successful professional learning communities and best practice in the management of teachers' well-being.

Lesson Study and real classrooms

A lesson is an organisational device used by teachers to bring students into contact with the curriculum in order to advance their development and achievement. Everyone is familiar with lessons. We have all experienced thousands of them as students. Almost everyone, it seems, has strong views on what constitutes a good lesson and is ever ready to tell teachers how to improve their work. This advice is very familiar to teachers. This is not surprising since the advice has been around for a very long time. The advice given to teachers currently is almost identical to the advice given in the 1850s.

There are, and have been for a hundred years, two broad schools of thought on how to improve lessons. In one view 'direct instruction' should be practised. Here, the teacher 'Begins the lesson with a short review of the prerequisite learning ... announces the goals of the lesson ... presents new material in short steps ... gives students practice after each step ... gives clear and detailed explanations ... and ensures a high level of active and successful practice' (Rosenshine and Stevens, 1986: 377).

In the alternate view, direct instruction is recognised as enhancing test results but at a severe cost. It limits students' understanding and their capacity to use and apply the routines and knowledge met. Material learned for tests under these conditions is very soon forgotten. The antidote, it is claimed, is to help students make the most of their capacities for discovery and thinking and in this way place their learning on a firm basis of deep comprehension.

In the public debates on schooling these two perspectives, 'direct instruction' and 'discovery learning' are cast as competing ideologies and as deadly foes. In the practice of most teachers they are seen as specific and useful tools in the pedagogic kit. Each tool affords different potentials for achieving different but symbiotic goals.

The challenge faced by teachers is less one to do with ideological preferences and much more to do with getting the tools to work in the complex setting of the classroom. The obvious challenges here are the huge amount of curriculum content to be covered, the vast diversity of relevant attributes amongst the students (including their prior attainment, their interests, values and attitudes, their state of health and their level of parental support) and the fact that the teacher is outnumbered 30 to 1 in most instances. Classrooms are far from ideal learning environments.

Studies of classroom life show that the teacher '... must attend to individual children whilst monitoring the rest of the class, supply corrective feedback whilst developing confidence and give children time to think whilst keeping one eye on the clock. The teacher distributes time to activities and attention and material resources to students. She organises movement about the room, the composition of groups and the flow of events' (Desforges and Cockburn, 1987: 15).

It has been estimated that primary grade teachers take part in 200–300 exchanges every hour of their working day (Jackson, 1968). Each exchange involves a unique mixture of personalities and circumstances. Various metaphors have been deployed to capture the teacher's classroom management activities. We have seen teacher as traffic cop, as ringmaster, or as quartermaster – each role seeking to impose order on a potentially chaotic situation. But each metaphor falls dangerously short of the requirements of classroom order which goes beyond mere discipline and control and necessitates a productive flow of work as a basis for student learning.

This is the context in which teachers must enhance their practice. CPD which takes place outside the classroom (i.e. the vast majority of CPD) assumes that lessons learned in training will be transformed and applied in the classroom. This is a high-risk assumption. The long history of research on knowledge application shows that transfer is the exception rather than the rule (Desforges, 1995). The challenge of learning skills in one context and using them in another is very well known amongst maths educators. What is perhaps less well known is that this is a general phenomenon. Transfer of training from the setting in which it is learned to a new setting happens only when the learner is extensively supported in the process with in-situ coaching. In the context of teachers' CPD this is a crucial matter (Duffy, 1993; Timperley, 2008).

One of the great, in-principle attractions of LS is that such transfer is unnecessary. CPD in the form of LS proceeds entirely in the teachers' classrooms and is entirely focused on an immediate challenge involving pupil progress.

Lesson Study and contemporary learning theory

A great deal is known about learning and the conditions that facilitate it. Bransford *et al.* (1999) offer a summary of relevant research that, in my view, has yet to be bettered. Bransford and his collaborators surveyed all the work on how humans learn and showed that the following circumstances should be provided for optimal learning progress.

The learning context should be learner-centred in the strict sense that it should start with what the learner already knows and build from there. Secondly, the learning setting should be intellectually challenging. It should require learners to think and to develop their powers of reflective thought. Third, the setting should provide feedback directly to inform and advance the development of performance.

We can see at a glance that LS perfectly meets these demanding criteria. Teachers engaged in LS start with an identification of a significant learning issue facing them. Collaboration focuses on thinking through students' current responses, desired responses and the design of appropriate interventions. The research model used in LS demands the collection and analysis of pertinent data on student engagement and progress. In short, LS is an ideal learning setting in terms of our best understanding of such.

Lesson Study and professional learning communities

Wiliam (2006) suggested that professional learning communities necessitate flexibility, choice, accountability and support in their design if they are to procure optimal outcomes for the professionals and their clients.

The first two features, flexibility and choice, stand in recognition of the fact that there is no 'one-size-fits-all' solution to the challenges of CPD. Teachers are as diverse in their training and learning needs as are their students. In this light, flexibility in regard to starting points and specific foci are essential. Learner choice is a direct corollary of this conclusion.

That said, there must be corporately valued outcomes from professional learning in terms of student progress. It follows that professional learning communities must be accountable to school leaders in these terms. By the same token, school leaders owe a reciprocal commitment to support and sustain professional development.

Again, it is clear at a glance that LS meets exactly these desiderata for professional learning communities. The participants, in the light of a careful analysis of their strengths and challenges, have considerable choice in regard to the detailed contents of their projects. At the same time there is a total commitment to promoting advances in student progress.

Finally, research reported here shows that LS, like learning communities everywhere, works only when soundly led and appropriately supported.

Lesson Study and staff well-being

Well-being is an ancient concept. Appearing in early history as a 'healthy mind in a healthy body' its modern form captures that sense each of us has to some degree of 'feeling good, doing fine, living well'. Over recent years a large research industry has been busy in pursuit of our understanding of the significance of the concept and of the factors which promote or inhibit its development. This is hardly the place to report and review this work. Those interested will find an excellent up to date review courtesy of the New Economic Foundation (2014). Perhaps one of the central findings of this review for school leaders is that well-being at work is one of the best available predictors of professional effectiveness.

It is also clear that some working conditions promote well-being (and hence effectiveness). People report higher levels of well-being when they work in small teams (as opposed to big groups or being on their own), when they have a degree of autonomy over their work (as opposed to being told what to do in detail and relentlessly) and when there are opportunities for creativity in the manner in which they attain desired goals.

Once again it is clear that LS meets all these criteria. Whilst the common and essential outcome for all LS is the improvement of pupil progress, there is a great deal of autonomy in the means by which this is achieved. Creativity is the *sine qua non* of LS. Small team working is a defining circumstance.

Of course all these features are risky for school leaders. There is an important accountability context. The risk, as will be seen in the work reported here, evaporates where LS is well led and where line managers in LS are well supported.

Summary

There is a compelling case for LS to be the CPD strategy of choice for the profession. LS has an ancient history and an excellent track record of success. Its operating principles are entirely at one with the conclusions drawn from research on how people learn. The management requirements are totally consistent with what we understand to be best practice in professional learning communities. Finally, LS procedures are in constructive alignment with the conditions which promote workers' well-being.

References

Bransford, J., Brown, A.L. and Cocking, R. (1999). *How People Learn.* Washington: National Academy Press.

Desforges, C. (ed.) (1995). *An Introduction to Teaching.* Oxford: Blackwell.

Desforges, C. and Cockburn, A. (1987). *Understanding the Mathematics Teacher.* Lewes: Falmer.

Desimone, L.M. (2011). A primer on effective professional development, R and D. *Phi Delta Kappan*, March: 68–71.

Duffy, G.G. (1993). Teachers progress to becoming expert strategy teachers. *The Elementary School Journal*, 94(2): 109–20.

Jackson, P. (1968). *Life in Classrooms.* New York: Holt.

New Economic Foundation (2014). Well-being at work: a review of the literature. www.nefconsulting.co.uk/well-being-at-work

Opfer, D.V. and Pedder, D. (2011). Conceptualising Teacher Professional Development. *Review of Educational Research*, 81: 376–403.

Rosenshine, B. and Stevens, K. (1986). Teaching Functions. In M.C. Wittrock (ed.) *Handbook of Research on Teaching.* New York: MacMillan, pp. 376–91.

Timperley, H. (2008). Teacher professional learning and development. International Academy of Education, www.ibe.unesco.org/publications.htm

Wiliam, D. (2006). Assessment: learning communities can use it to engineer a bridge between teaching and learning. *Journal of Staff Development*, 27(1): 16–20.

Acknowledgements

I would like to thank the many school leaders and teachers with whom I have worked over the 13 years that I have been developing Lesson Study. I would like to thank all the contributors to this book and especially Charles Desforges for his helpful comments on drafts. I would like to thank Sally Walsh and Jo Cottrell, two school leaders who contributed their valuable views and time to my research and who helped me to begin to understand what is important in leading Lesson Study. And finally, I would like to thank Jacquie Freeman for her help in preparing this manuscript.

Chapter 1

How Lesson Study works and why it creates excellent learning and teaching

Peter Dudley

I agree with Charles Desforges in his Foreword that Lesson Study (LS) is an approach to continuing professional development (CPD) that schools should adopt. There is a lot to commend it and to evidence its distinctive impact compared with other forms of CPD as you will read within these pages. Studies of how LS is being used to best effect and of how it helps teachers, leaders, schools and colleges to adjust or modify their practices in order to afford more learning are important. The medical trials currently ongoing in educational research in England as I write (and which I will reference below) will I am sure add to our understanding about how LS works. But for the reasons given by Professor Desforges in the preceding pages and for reasons that will unfold in this chapter and those that follow, I believe that LS is not only the CPD strategy of choice for schools, but that it also lends itself to use across schools and beyond schools as they collaborate and learn together with their university, college and other partners. LS is clearly emerging as professional learning for our time.

The purpose of this book is to give you a taste of how LS works in some schools and school systems and some knowledge of how to get going with and to lead LS. It also provides some evidence of how and why LS works and how it can help you to enhance learning, enhance schools, enhance initial and continuing teacher education, and to enhance curriculum, assessment, leadership and the system as a whole. The book provides insights from the UK, Japan and China, as well as a global perspective.

Amongst the book's intended audience, then, are leaders of schools and local school systems and alliances, those in leadership positions in higher or continuing education as well as all those who work with and lead teacher development.

The book will give you more than enough knowledge to lead LS developments from any of these contexts. Now, I could save you a read by confessing that in my experience the best way to learn about LS is to get stuck in and do it – but if you read this book first you will do so more successfully.

In this first chapter I will provide a background to LS, what it is, how it works to promote deep teacher learning that change practice and improves learning for pupils and in particular how it is developing in the UK. I will then briefly introduce the chapters that follow.

1 What is Lesson Study and why does it work?

I was recently reviewing a video of a group of three teachers who were working together in a LS group. They were discussing a 'research lesson' (see page 8) that one of them had just taught and which had been observed by the other two members of the LS group. They discussed the way that the pupils had learned and compared this with how they had predicted that the pupils would learn when they had been planning the research lesson together. They explored the reasons why particular pupils had found aspects of the lesson difficult or easy and as they did so – raising hypotheses, testing out ideas, modifying, challenging and qualifying their ideas and suggestions – they gradually formed some tentative theories about how they could help the children to learn more successfully another time. They seamlessly moved into planning the next research lesson in which they were going to apply some of the things that they had learned from this group analysis of the lesson they had just conducted and to test out some of their theories.

They were deeply, deeply engrossed; absorbed in collectively solving the riddles of how to help these *real* pupils in a *real* class to learn about multiplying and dividing fractions more effectively and with greater understanding of what they were doing and why.

It was clear to me that all three teachers cared deeply about helping these children – even though only one of them regularly taught this class. It was clear that during the research lesson these teachers had found things out about the ways some of the pupils were learning that they had not known before. And it was clear that they were drawing on all the knowledge and experience that they collectively possessed about mathematics, about teaching mathematics, about how twelve year olds learn mathematics (or don't learn) and that they were also drawing more broadly on their experience and knowledge about what motivates children of this age to learn, about pedagogy, about teaching and, above all, about learning.

As I watched, I too became rapidly engrossed in their discussion – puzzling along with these three teachers about how to help a group of pupils not become confused about the difference between multiplying and dividing fractions. I wondered and hypothesised with them as they pieced together their conclusions from the research lesson and started to use them to plan their next research lesson. And I was as excited as they were about what would happen in that lesson: to what extent the ideas that they were tweaking and honing and then retrying in that next research lesson would bear fruit in helping these children to learn more effectively.

It was only as they were packing up and talking about what was scheduled for the following day that I realised how much time had passed. They had started discussing the lesson in daylight and now the windows were black and the room was illuminated only by the classroom lights. I dragged the cursor back to the beginning of the video and fast-forwarded through it again. I watched them speedily, jerkily, earnestly talking, laughing, crowding round the planner, frowning, nodding, writing – all in fast motion. And sure enough, this time I noticed the light outside the windows fading. I saw the classroom lights take over. But then I saw a cleaner enter the classroom with a trolley of equipment and move from table to table squirting cleaner onto the surfaces and wiping them down – working awkwardly around the LS group who carried on with their discussions heedless of her presence. And I realised that whilst I had watched the video the first time at normal speed, that cleaner had been as oblivious to me as she had been to the group she sprayed and wiped around, because I too had been so completely focused on their discussions.

Then – still in fast motion and still with the LS teachers frenetically discussing, gesticulating, absorbed and unaware of the cleaner's arrival and departure – I saw through the classroom window a light go on in the adjacent classroom as the cleaner worked her way methodically around that room, and then a further two classrooms in the block before returning for her trolley and leaving.

The LS group had been in intensive, sustained, unbroken group discussion about their pupils and about these two (one past and one future) research lessons, for over an hour.

Over the past 25 years I have used many models of teacher learning with countless groups of teachers and in many different contexts. But I know of only one approach that has never failed to elicit the depth of learning, the detailed accountability of teachers *to how real children are learning in real classrooms* and, as a result, that has never failed to elicit profound changes in subsequent practice.

LS as an approach to teacher learning

So while Charles Desforges, in the Foreword to this book, is of course correct when he says that for pupils the classroom is far from the ideal learning environment, I now argue, paradoxically perhaps, that for teachers, the classroom *can* be an ideal learning environment. But this is only when the classroom is occupied by a LS group of teachers planning their research lesson; or when it is filled with adults and children, as teachers teach and observe pupils learning during that research lesson; or again when it has emptied once more after the research lesson save for the LS group, intense in their discussion (and of course the occasional cleaner). In this discussion, the group members reflect upon the research lesson that has just taken place, sharing and analysing their observation notes and data, raising their hypotheses about how the children had learned or why some of them failed to learn as predicted, and speculating about what could have been done differently. They then begin to piece together the elements of their next research lesson, painstakingly applying to it their findings from this last one as they do so.

LS is the world's fastest growing approach to teacher learning, and to developing teaching that in turn improves pupil learning. It has transformed the practice of tens of thousands of teachers and educational professionals worldwide – myself included!

LS has its roots in Japan, where it has been practiced by Japanese teachers for 140 years or more. And since the beginning of the twenty-first century LS has become a global phenomenon. LS allows teachers to transform the way they teach the children they are teaching *now* in the lessons they are teaching *now*. It takes place in their classrooms. It enables them to problem solve and to share their practices, to understand each others' pupils' learning and each others' teaching; and through this to learn from and with each other.

LS provides a context where teachers can take risks with their practice and feel safe to share their reciprocal, professional vulnerabilities. It gets to the parts that other professional development doesn't reach!

LS works because it allows teachers to see, share, tap into and learn from usually invisible stores of tacit professional knowledge that are normally inaccessible as a learning resource. It allows the inexperienced to learn from the experienced, the generalist to learn from the expert – but also the reverse of these.

LS requires no special equipment or resources. It requires minimal training – the best way to get good at it is to do it. And LS is currently not only improving learning and teaching, it is improving schools and raising standards.

What is LS?

LS is a deceptively simple sequence of collaborative reflective practice (Pollard *et al.*, 2014): joint professional development or 'JPD' as David Hargreaves (2012) terms it. The beauty of its simplicity is that any small group of teachers can do it. Because it requires no technology or prior experience, it is now in use in many developing countries worldwide. But the list of countries now using LS now includes all the top performing nations as well. The danger in the simplicity of LS, however, is that it is easily adapted and corrupted by a teaching profession that too often has been encouraged simply to innovate for innovation's sake, to play fast and loose with an 'adapt adopt' approach to practice transfer and which even in the twenty-first century, is still unused to adopting professional levels of clinical discipline when applying and honing classroom interventions or innovations.

The LS cycle

I will set out the sequence of a lesson study here. This and later chapters will help you to build a broader understanding of what makes a lesson study a 'lesson study'; what liberties can be taken with its design without harming its power, and what seemingly harmless adaptations can render the resulting process one so weakened that it should not be termed LS.

In LS a group of teachers work together to improve the learning of their pupils and to develop ways of teaching them that help them to overcome barriers or difficulties they are encountering in learning, often in learning some very specific aspects of the curriculum.

In the model of LS that I have developed over the last 14 years in the UK and which features significantly in this book, teachers involved have a clear focus for this improvement in their pupils' learning. I will give two different examples. The improvement could be:

i   to help some pupils who are not making the progress their teachers feel they could be making. The focus here being on particular pupils' levels of engagement or motivation or other factors affecting the way that they engage with learning.

Or it could be:

ii   to introduce a curriculum unit on ratio to a particular class with more success than in the past – because teachers have noticed that many pupils do not make as much progress in this unit as they do in most other mathematics units. The focus here is on curriculum and pedagogy.

In order to create the conditions necessary for teachers to learn together, LS group teachers usually adopt a LS group protocol (see Panel 1 below) that ensures they can work together and quickly develop trust in each other, thus then feeling safe to take risks or to get things wrong, and so that all the group members are equal as learners in the group.

Panel I A Lesson Study (LS) Group Protocol

This protocol exists to help create common expectations amongst the LS group members. In doing this it will help the group to form a good working relationship that helps members to share ideas, concerns, challenges and 'wonderings' without fear of criticism. All this will aid the sharing and discovery of new practice knowledge.

At all stages in this LS we will act according to the following:

- all members of the LS group are equal as learners whatever their age, experience, expertise or seniority in school (or beyond)
- all contributions are treated with unconditional positive regard – this does not mean they will not be subject to analysis, doubt or challenge, it means no one will be made to feel foolish for venturing a suggestion. It is often suggestions that make you feel foolish or vulnerable that are of the greatest value and generate the most learning
- we will support whoever teaches the research lesson(s) and make faithful observations recording as much as possible what pupils say as well as do

- we will use common tools for lesson study – planners, pupil interview prompts and approaches to sharing outcomes with each other
- we will use pupils' work and their interview comments to inform the post lesson discussion alongside our observations
- we will use the post lesson discussion flow starting by discussing what each case pupil did compared with what we predicted and let the discussion flow from there
- we will listen to each other and to ourselves when we speak and build on the discussion making suggestions, raising hypotheses, elaborating, qualifying and at all times being accountable to our lesson aims, our case pupils and our observation and other research lesson data
- we will share what we learn – our new practice knowledge – with our colleagues as accurately and vividly as we can in such a way that they can benefit from and try it out themselves
- we will share the aims and outcomes of our lesson study with our pupils appropriately depending on their ages and stages of development. Their views, ideas and perspectives will be treated with equally positive regard.

Signed and dated by LS group members.

Source: Dudley, P. (2014). *Lesson Study: a handbook*. Cambridge: LSUK. http://lessonstudy.co.uk/lesson-study-a-handbook/

2 What happens in a Lesson Study

Research lessons

LS group members will teach a number (usually three) 'research lessons' or 'study lessons' which they plan together having done some research on what approaches might motivate the pupils in example i (above) to become more engaged or which might reveal how other schools are achieving better progress in teaching ratio as in example ii (above).

They plan each research lesson with three particular pupils in mind. These are 'case pupils' (Dudley, 2003, 2013; Chichibu, 2014). They may be three of those pupils whose engagement and progress is a

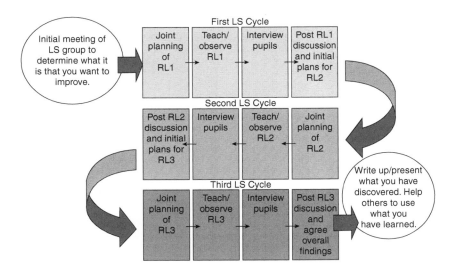

Figure 1.1 A typical lesson study with three research lesson (RL) cycles
Source: Dudley, P. (2011). *The Lesson Study Toolkit.* Bethlehem: Bethlehem University.

concern to the teachers as in example i, or they might simply be one of the higher attaining pupils in mathematics in the class, one of the lower attainers and one who typifies the middle attaining group (which would be more likely to be the case in example ii).

As they plan each of these research lessons together these teachers are thinking about how each of their case pupils might respond at different stages of the lesson. They agree together what they would expect to see in the responses of each case pupil at different stages of the lesson if it is running successfully for that pupil. These predictions play an important role in the research lessons.

As a result of this attention to predicting the likely learning behaviours of each case pupil in the research lesson, LS groups in the UK often use a research lesson planner based on the format given in Figure 1.2.

Conducting research lessons

Once the research lesson planning is complete, the LS group teaches the lesson together. One member will lead the teaching while the others act as observers. But there is a key difference in what LS group observers watch, record and make judgements about and what has traditionally

Research lesson planning, observation and discussion sheet	Subject		Learning Focus		Teacher/observer	

Precisely what is this research lesson aiming to teach? (it may be a section of a longer teaching sequence) *By the end of this lesson pupils will be able to.......... and we will know this when...*

What learning or teaching technique is the research lesson aiming to develop? *We are hoping to improve...*

Current attainment and success criteria Describe what you are looking for from them by end of lesson in the identified aspect	Case pupil A......................... Success criterion for this focus		Case pupil B......................... Success criterion for this focus		Case pupil C......................... Success criterion for this focus	
Stage of lesson sequence	How you predict case pupil A will respond	*How they are observed to respond*	How you predict case pupil B will respond	*How they are observed to respond*	How you predict case pupil C will respond	*How they are observed to respond*	Patterns/issues
Stage... (approximate time)						
Stage... (approximate time)						
Final stage... (approximate time)						
What were they able to do? (What progress have they made and how do you know?)						
Initial thoughts						

Figure 1.2 Research Lesson Observation and Discussion Template

Source: Dudley, P. (2014). *Lesson Study: a handbook*. Cambridge: LSUK. http://lessonstudy.co.uk/lesson-study-a-handbook/

happened in lesson observations in classrooms in England for the past 20 or so years at least.

Observing learning rather than observing teaching

Instead of using a pre-prepared checklist or an Ofsted Evidence Form to make observation notes on the teacher's teaching, LS group members use a copy of the research lesson plan (see Figure 1.2) and, rather than commenting on teaching, they instead compare what pupil learning they had predicted would happen with what they observed did happen.

So rather than observing teaching, they observe *pupils learning* in the context of being taught. This process of jointly observing learning in the context of teaching and learning in a lesson is the essence of LS.

This focus on learning in a context of being taught in a lesson is also at the heart of LS's popularity with teachers and its power to improve and change practice. It doesn't matter if something goes wrong because the lesson belongs to the group, not to any individual. Furthermore, by observing pupils learning, the LS group builds up a detailed picture of the effect of the research lesson on pupils' thinking and cognition. This helps the teachers to understand what the pupils did and did not understand, what assumptions about the pupils had been wrong in the first place and in what ways the pupils had interpreted the lesson's content or behaved in ways that had not been predicted by the group. Such a wealth of highly detailed information fuels productive analysis and informs subsequent revisions of the pedagogical or curricular approaches being developed, in great detail and depth.

This is of course is in marked contrast with what we are used to as a profession. Traditionally, lesson observation in England has involved observer 'experts' watching teachers teach and making interpretive judgements about the effectiveness of this teaching: ('effectiveness' here meaning the impact of the teaching on the learning of the pupils). Such observations have been the backbone of Ofsted inspection since 1993 and teachers' performance management arrangements since the late 1980s. Both processes claim to improve teaching. But no one really uses these 'opportunities' to explore the areas of practice about which they have least confidence. Instead, in performance management contexts people tend to teach something they are reasonably confident will be unproblematic or better, and then go through the motions with their appraiser of agreeing a target for improvement but in fact leaving untouched the real areas where improvement in their teaching is needed.

Teachers in LS groups consistently report that the relationships that form between their members lead to the kind of deep, engrossed focus on improving learning for real pupils that I observed in the video described above and also lead them to work collectively on areas of practice about which the group members are less than confident. They also report that they feel safe to take risks together to improve their teaching and practice-knowledge in these areas of lower confidence and performance.

Discussing and analysing the research lessons.

In accordance with LS's focus on pupils rather than on teaching, LS groups always discuss the learning of the case pupils one after another before discussing the teaching. This is the post research lesson discussion protocol (see Figure 1.3). This also helps to keep the focus on the pupils' learning and away from aspects of the teaching, unless these aspects are specifically related to the pupils' learning or mis-learning in the particular research lesson.

It is striking that, almost without exception, every LS group I have worked with over a 13-year period has always found that after their first research lesson, they discover that at least one (and frequently more than one) of their case pupils had been learning in a very different way from those predicted in the group's LS plan. This is either because they have been poorly assessed or, probably more usually, because teachers had formed a particular view of the pupil and about what he or she is capable of achieving. Such views can come to replace active, ongoing understanding of a pupil. They can even become stereotypical, distorted by the pupils' reputation or over influenced by particular behaviours exhibited by the pupil. Yet in such cases it is this distorted and out of

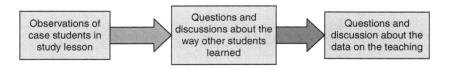

Figure 1.3 Post research lesson discussion protocol

Source: Dudley, P. (2014). *Lesson Study: a handbook*. Cambridge: LSUK. http://lesson-study.co.uk/lesson-study-a-handbook/

date view that continues to inform the learning that is being planned for this pupil each day.

The strict discipline of a research lesson however, where the learning of pupils is predicted and then observed in practice, has the power to expose the way pupils' learning behaviours can differ markedly from those assumed by their teachers. And, as stated above, LS often does so.

When teachers discover, confront and examine these issues as they arise in a lesson study, they are usually lead to reappraise their understandings of how they think about particular pupils (or groups of pupils) and about the learning of these pupils and this therefore changes how they subsequently think about teaching and assessment.

I investigated the features of teacher learning in LS that promote such forms of learning by identifying these phenomena in the discussions of LS groups planning and analysing research lessons. I did this by recording these meetings and analysing their discourse at interaction level. I discovered many moments of reappraisal – and sometimes of acceptance or adoption of new knowledge that was subsequently incorporated by teachers into reappraised and reformed practice. 'Teacher learning points' is the term I gave to the moments in their discussion when teachers began to question and then to reappraise their practice and gradually to see the sense in adopting the revised approach. They occurred mostly when teachers were hypothesising together about how children might learn in a section of a lesson being planned, or about how they had or had not learned in a research lesson just observed. During these teacher learning points, the teachers were drawing upon a wealth of very different kinds of knowledge that they possessed between them.

> Teachers drew upon knowledge of pupils and knowledge of pedagogy at [teacher] learning points in both studies, but the most common association by far was with Pedagogical Content Knowledge.[1] ... LS group members are held [to account] by the level of detail required in their planning and analysis discussions, [which] forces even tiny differences of view about practice or content to become exposed. The group needs then to resolve the cognitive dissonance thus created between group members in order to address collectively the needs of the pupils in the imagined or re-imagined lesson, and these represent points of teacher learning.
>
> (Dudley, 2013: 118)

Section 4 (below) illustrates in greater detail how the discipline of making visible their assumptions about pupil learning, as well as their observations of that learning in practice, amongst the LS group helps these teachers to see their pupils with new eyes and to make changes to teaching and curriculum which would not otherwise have been possible.

Passing on to other professionals the learning from a lesson study

Because we tend to teach in isolation in the West (with the exception of teaching assistants for some) we have not become used to other teaching professionals engaging with us in our teaching, planning or assessments. This makes it difficult to talk about our practice. Once qualified, we virtually never see ourselves teach.

But isolated practice is not the biggest threat to our profession's abilities to understand and therefore be able to change our classroom practice. Successive studies (Wragg *et al.*, 1996; Arnot *et al.*, 2004) have shown how the busy-ness of classrooms makes it impossible to see most of what is happening in them at any one time. I will explain more about this in the following section.

3 How Lesson Study came West

LS is influenced by the Chinese tradition of public teaching which remains a feature of education in China (Chen, 2011) and also in many of the countries that have come under Chinese influence in the region. LS, however, is usually more collaborative than 'public'. It is a way of life for teachers in Japan and it only became the subject of international interest in the late 1990s when Western countries – and the United States in particular – were exploring what they could learn from Japan's consistent high performance in international comparative studies such as Trends in International Mathematics and Science Study (TIMSS) and Programme for International Student Assessment (PISA). They discovered the phenomenon of LS (Stigler and Hiebert, 1999) and the deep, collective understanding that Japanese teachers and schools seem to have about how their pupils are learning and how they can help them to improve, which was in marked contrast to much of what is experienced in state education systems in the West.

In Chapter 2 of this book, Haiyan Xu and David Pedder give an authoritative review of the process as evidenced through the literature, from the early roots of LS right up to the present day.

Researchers and teacher educators like Catherine Lewis, a Japanese-speaking American educator, began introducing LS in the late 1990s (Lewis, 1998). It has since spread across the globe. I conducted my first LS in 2001 in Ilford, London and LS has since grown steadily in use in the UK. It is now firmly located as the teacher development model in a number of high profile programmes across very many teaching school alliances and in increasing numbers of schools, initial teacher training programmes and higher degrees. Currently there are several publicly funded and sizeable development and research programmes underway across the UK[2] focused on LS. They range from randomised quasi medical trials investigating impact in core subjects or the efficacy of LS as a means of closing achievement gaps, to locality-based development and research programmes such as the London Schools Excellence Fund programme led by Camden Council, London and the University of Cambridge exploring how LS can be used to improve pupil learning and teacher expertise in teaching higher order mathematics.

4 The impact of Lesson Study on school results

In between 2008 and 2011 Leading Teachers in the Primary National Strategy (Dudley, 2012) began to use a LS-based approach to their work with Year 6 (10 to 11 year olds) teachers in schools described at the time as 'coasting' schools where attainment was average or above but where pupils were making poor progress between ages 8 and 11 and should really have been attaining at higher levels. They worked with these Year 6 teachers during four visits and supported them in conducting one cycle of three research lessons: a LS in English or mathematics. When the test results in English and mathematics of the schools in which the leading teachers used the LS-based approach were compared with the results of other coasting schools where the leading teachers had not used the LS-based approach, the gains seen in the LS-based schools were double those of the others which had themselves improved at a higher rate than had been the case nationally.

While this comparison is far from a randomised clinical trial, it does indicate considerable gains across a large number of schools that used LS: gains that were larger than those in schools where the intervention was not LS based. It was also large scale – in fact it could be argued that it was 'at scale'. There were around 900 Leading Teachers at the time across England, funded by the Department of Education to provide this support to coasting schools and they were trained in doing so by my teams at the National Strategies, led by Jean Lang and supported by Gill Jordan who are both contributors to this book. Similar gains are reported by Hadfield *et al.* (2011) in their independent evaluation of the National Strategies' Primary Leading Teacher programme.

But even though we have yet to discover the precise 'effects' of LS on pupil attainment and progress, we do know a considerable amount more now than we did five years ago about the impact of LS on teachers' practice knowledge and subsequent classroom teaching as well as on their assessment of pupils. I will use the next section of this chapter to present the findings of research into the impact of LS on teacher learning that subsequently improves pupils learning.

5 How Lesson Study works to improve teachers' practice

The Japanese say a lesson is like a 'swiftly flowing river' (Lewis, 1998). This metaphor conjures up an image of a teacher as a canoeist who has plotted a path through this 'swiftly flowing river' through their lesson plan. From a distance the river looks beautiful, sparkling in the sunshine, but as you lower the boat, the strength and complexities of the currents and eddies become clearer. Once in the water the canoeist is mostly at the mercy of these currents. While he or she can use the paddle and physical strength to negotiate their planned path as best as they can, the currents constantly pull the canoe off its path. One is never fully in control of the boat in such circumstances. And a teacher can never perfectly predict how a lesson will unfold.

A teacher confronted with 30 or more human brains, each a complex, swiftly moving data source, each interpreting the lesson slightly or sometimes very differently from the others in the classroom – and doing so for the most part invisibly – can do little more than the canoeist: judge and ride the currents intervening where he or she can in order to negotiate a way through the lesson that produces as much learning as possible while constantly responding to unexpected feedback or misconceptions.

A teacher sees no more of the learning that has gone on in their lesson than the canoeist sees of the parts of the river not directly encountered. Most of the interventions that a teacher makes in a lesson, like the paddle strokes of the canoeist, will be made automatically, unconsciously, in response to unpredicted turns that the lesson has taken for different pupils. A few interventions will be in response to conscious thoughts that the teacher has as he or she converses with or observes pupils whose misconceptions are becoming evident or who need feedback in order to progress to the next stage – but most will be invisible, automatic and unconscious.

We remember the conscious interventions. We are not aware we are making the unconscious ones and we cannot remember them in our conscious memory. So unless we find a way of accessing this tacit knowledge and sharing it with colleagues we will take most of our professional knowledge to our graves.

Tacit knowledge and teacher learning in LS

I have found evidence, however, that LS does precisely that. The findings from my robust but small-scale study (Dudley, 2013) are now being investigated in a much larger study being conducted in a much larger scale development and research programme led by the London Borough of Camden and the University of Cambridge.[3]

In my study LS groups recorded themselves planning research lessons and discussing them afterwards. The research revealed that the deliberate, recursive process of LS where teachers move from planning, to research lesson, to post-lesson discussion and through successive cycles that follow this pattern creates conditions where they feel safe to take risks, explore areas of low confidence and engage in micro-level planning and analysis of small teaching sequences as described in Section 1 above. It also builds a sense of community amongst LS group members. Figure 1.4 illustrates how the jointly imagined lesson from the planning phase, the jointly experienced research lesson from the observation and teaching phase and the subject of the post-lesson discussion combine to promote the conditions necessary for learning as set out in socio-cultural learning theory. Through this dialectic of imagined and experienced learning, LS creates many of the components of learning that are described through socio-cultural learning theory. They include the building of community and the suppression of concerns about one's self within the group, and the creation of collaborative 'interthinking' through a shared 'intermental zone' of thought where ideas can be shared and developed by the group (Mercer, 2004) through social interaction and in which participants build shared perspectives as a result of each member understanding the perspective of the others' thoughts which is known as intersubjectvity.

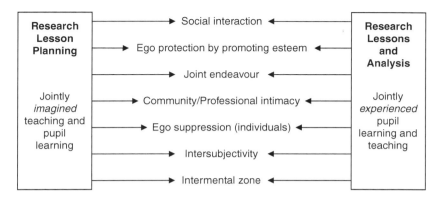

Figure 1.4 How planning, experiencing and analysing research lessons contribute to aspects of teacher learning in LS

Source: Dudley, P. (2011). Lessons for learning: how teachers learn in contexts of Lesson Study. PhD thesis, University of Cambridge.

Teachers learning through talk in LS

All of the above is achieved through discussion and dialogue. Talk! Learning's 'tool of tools' (Vygotsky, 1986). But in LS groups teachers go beyond the uses of talk most commonly seen in work-based learning.

When planning or analysing research lessons, LS group members frequently try out sequences of teacher talk *in role* as if they were the teacher in the classroom teaching the lesson. They will modify each other's suggestions by going into role themselves and offering an alternative suggested question, instruction or phrase. In the example below, three teachers are planning to develop reflective diary writing with a class of nine year olds, extending some of the less engaged boys by helping them to write in role as an Iceni 'chariot mechanic' who is serving one of Boudicca's charioteers in a great battle with the Romans.

The LS group members slip in and out of role as they rehearse what they might say to the class as they model being in role themselves and gradually bring the pupils into play as well by imagining how they might react.

LLOYD: Or … The drama could be … a post-battle review. You know what … All the troops coming back together. What went well. Why we didn't win or why did we lose so many…

YASMIN: Could we talk about 'why' with the teacher in role as Boudicca? You could put yourself in role as Boudicca and get the children all in role as ... chariot (tries to think of a work for chariot technicians)...

LLOYD: 'mechanics' (smiling)

YASMIN: Chariot mechanics (chuckles). And they could come back and tell you about the day and their success or otherwise?

LLOYD: ...and you could say...

YASMIN: (Interrupting) I mean not in terms of the success or the loss but in terms of the actual state of the chariots and er ... You know from that perspective?

LLOYD: I mean you could really, you know, force the issue couldn't you. 'Why did this wheel fall off when I was in the middle of a town?' or you know 'I want to congratulate you for preparing such an excellent chariot. How did you do it?'

YASMIN: 'My horse only lasted ten minutes. What happened? Had you fed it?'

KEITH: Mm to to make it different as well. You need to ... We need to take them on a journey, you know. 'Its taken us three months to get to the battle site.' You know. Travelling all the way to – wherever this battle is...

YASMIN: Yes

KEITH: You are ... 'We are already hungry and tired and I, I don't know if I can get enough hay for my horse.' Um. 'The big battle is tomorrow.' You know, set it up that way so 'We've got the big battle. Now describe the state you're in already' and, you know, 'think about what you've got to do to get your horse and chariot ready' and urm. And then you can say 'Now. The battle has happened. Your horse and chariot has come back' ... Hopefully!...

In another quite different context Rose and Wanda try out different phrasings as they explore in role how these might sound to their class of nine year olds who are learning about counting across zero with positive and negative numbers.

WANDA: And just talk about 'Although they look bigger it's actually smaller the further away from zero it is. If I add I'm getting closer to zero. If I take away I'm actually getting further away from zero'...

WANDA: ...I probably would even differentiate ... 'No all of us do those together' or kind of (clicks fingers) or 'Do these five sums'. Bring them all back. Check the misconceptions. Check they are using the number line appropriately. I mean especially with zero. Things like that, and then say 'Okay, If you want a little bit more practice, have a go with these. If you think you're ready for a bit of a challenge, try to do some of these bigger numbers'. So at the same time they can practice some doing bigger numbers.[And again a few seconds later.]

ROSE: [To Wanda] How will we show a negative number? [To an imaginary class] How will you plot this negative number?' [Suggesting in role]

WANDA: [A is writing all this down so the dialogue is slow] [Also to an imaginary class] 'Can you give a number larger than minus fifteen ... but that's smaller than...?'

The 'learning points' (Dudley, 2013), at which it is discernable within a teacher's talk that he or she is beginning to change a belief about his or her practice or beginning to adopt a new practice, are critical moments in teacher learning. Teachers will often hold long-held practices dear to them, even in the face of evidence of improved pupil learning resulting from an alternative approach. This may be because adopting a new practice makes one feel guilty about having used less effective practice in the past but it is usually because change is effortful and unnerving.

In my analysis of teacher learning points (Dudley, 2013) I looked for the kinds of conversational interactions in which they were most likely to occur. I found that the interaction type that is most frequently generative of a teacher learning point is *hypothesising*. When teachers are raising and testing hypotheses about what might improve a pupil's learning or what might have improved a pupil's learning in a lesson just observed, teachers tend to have their minds open to changes in belief and practice. They put these changes into practice in subsequent research lessons and report building many of them into their own classroom teaching. LS generates more hypothesising in its exploratory talk sequences than almost all other interaction types and so LS is rich linguistic and cognitive ground for teacher learning points to occur. When a teacher encounters a similar learning point several times in the course of a LS during the three research lessons, that teacher's practice and professional knowledge can be profoundly changed – as ultimately was Rose's in the above example (see Dudley, 2013).

Sharing the knowledge and insights gained in a LS so that others might use it

As a footnote to this section, it is worth reminding ourselves that, traditionally, lesson studies are passed on so that others can use the knowledge and insights gained in the lesson studies in order to achieve gains in their own classrooms. The 'passing on' can take the form of a structured conversation with colleagues, a presentation in a staff meeting, writing up a case study and posting it on the school's intranet. Or it can be more active and in keeping with the learning design of LS itself. You might invite colleagues into your classroom to observe you using the technique and then discuss it with these colleagues and the pupils afterwards. Or one could go the whole hog and keep the entire class for an hour after school, set up the classroom in the sports hall and perform the lesson with the approaches you have developed in front of an invited audience of staff from neighbouring schools, universities and other advisory organisations. The Japanese call such events 'public research lessons' and you will need to make sure you have a 'roving microphone' ready for the post-lesson discussion with members of the audience and pupils. A number of schools in the UK now regularly feature such events in their professional learning calendars.

There are two spin offs to all of these matters that relate to quality and long-term impact on learning for pupils and teachers. Evidence from my research (Dudley, 2013) suggests that teachers who plan their lesson studies in the knowledge and expectation that they will be presenting the findings to their peers consciously raise their game. They are more ambitious and more accountable to peers – and consequently their lesson studies can be of greater quality. But the act of presenting one's lesson study – of advocating for the knowledge and insights one has gained – seems also to 'fix' the new practice more permanently in one's subsequent teaching. Newly innovated practice is always more effortful to reproduce than ingrained practice, and for the first few times it can be more nerve wracking. These feelings can lead teachers to revert to former ingrained practices, even though they have clear evidence that they are not as effective. Giving teachers opportunities to share their LS findings can, therefore, profoundly affect the long-term impact of the LS on pupil outcomes and teaching quality for years to come.

Rehearsed, imagined classroom dialogue: tacit knowledge and teacher learning

Perhaps the most striking finding of all from this research was the fact that the kind of conversational interaction most frequently associated with learning points after hypothesising was *rehearsed lesson dialogue* of the kind exemplified in the transcripts above. And as there were far fewer occurrences of rehearsed lesson dialogue than there were of hypothesising, the relationship with learning points was arguably stronger.

This suggests that going into role as teacher within the LS group allows teachers to experience the feel of the classroom as it might be and to listen to the rehearsed dialogue with the ears of teacher and pupil. This in turn allows the natural, tacit knowledge responses to surface that would normally come to a teacher as 'second nature' in a lesson context. These are almost impossible to access when away from that classroom context as I have discussed above. But this evidence suggests that 'in role' such knowledge can surface and that all members of the LS group can engage with and contribute to it – in role in their imagined lesson.

This is very important. But we know little about tacit knowledge. We know that it has the power to keep us upright on bicycles while our conscious minds work out the route we need to follow and watch the traffic, or to allow our fingers to play complex music on an instrument thus freeing our conscious minds to concentrate on the overall performance and the conductor. And we know that even if we do not utilise the tacit knowledge for a long period we can still summon it up the moment, years later, when we get back on a bicycle and ride it as if we had been on it only yesterday (…'like riding a bike').

We know a few other things about tacit knowledge that are resonant with LS. For example, we know that it is stored and retrieved very differently from conscious, propositional knowledge; we know that it is easier to access in face to face contexts where people trust each other and have reciprocal relationships – each depending on and benefiting from the others; and we know that it is important in developing innovative thought (Koskinen and Vanharanta, 2002; Koskinen *et al.*, 2003; Erden *et al.*, 2008; Gopesh *et al.*, 2010). Paradoxically, we also know that if we try to encourage the use of tacit knowledge through reward systems (Hau *et al.*, 2013), the results are counter productive – as every tennis player who has ever needed a first serve for the match knows!

The more you consciously think about the first service you have delivered a thousand times, the more you cannot perform it.

LS group members repeatedly report that the conditions that they experience in LS groups are congruent with those that are supportive of tacit knowledge use, as are the deliberative reflexive processes of the LS cycle (Dudley, 2011).

It may be that LS's abilities to conjure up and make accessible tacit knowledge so effectively is what sets it apart from much other collaborative teacher learning and enquiry models.

The shared experience, knowledge and purpose that LS groups build together also build motivation and lessen feelings of vulnerability. As they get to know the pupils and their colleagues their care and passion to help the pupils and their colleagues – the group – to succeed grow stronger. While in the meetings planning the first research lesson LS group members can still feel nervous, exposed or vulnerable, the experience of teaching and observing a lesson together reveals the reciprocal nature of that vulnerability and binds them together. Their focus on the pupils and their ideas of how to help them to learn more effectively grow with each research lesson as they understand the pupils and the effects of their teaching in more depth. And usually by the third or fourth research lesson, they have scented success – and are testing out an approach that will not only help the pupils in this LS, but which could be adapted and generalised from for use with others elsewhere.

For this reason it is vital to utilise this gain from the sequence of research lessons. The knowledge generated in the third research lesson in a sequence is usually much richer in depth, insight and replicability than the first. So while it is tempting to conduct LS 'one research lesson at a time' with no clear sequence (managing the sequences of three takes planning and commitment as we hear from school leaders in Chapter 3), the outcomes are likely to be more expensive overall and of less value (Dudley, 2011).

6 Sharing learning from Lesson Study: a global movement?

LS has the beauty of being a process that is portable, easy to replicate and cheap, as well as highly generative of improved classroom outcomes for pupils and improved knowledge of pupils' learning, of successful teaching approaches and of pedagogical content knowledge for teachers.

These properties also make it a powerful transfer agent, capable of mobilising teacher practice knowledge which is notoriously difficult to move even from one classroom to another, let alone between schools, school systems or between countries around the world.

Studies such as the McKinsey reports (McKinsey, 2007; Mourshed *et al.*, 2010) have underscored the importance of such approaches to making classroom practice visible in such ways as they can be mobilised laterally from teacher to teacher and school to school in the course of the organisation's 'business as usual' or 'standard operating' procedures. There is a revolution taking place in the UK as a result – spurred on by the creation of peer to peer 'teaching schools', and university training schools alongside the removal of government school improvement agencies, the national assessment framework and reductions in the local improvement functions of councils and even university education departments.

Web-based platforms are beginning to act as trading stations for lesson studies. These include voluntary organisations such as my own www.lessonstudy.co.uk which is visited by thousands each month from across the world interested in downloading resources and lesson studies – or indeed in posting their own. They include charities such as www.teacherdevelopmenttrust.org which runs web-based LS coaching through its national teacher enquiry network. They also include UK universities (such as University of Leicester), a growing number of which have practice sharing and information sites for lesson studies, and, further afield, organisations like the Chicago Lesson Study Group and Mills College, Oakland, California, which have been instrumental in helping people to access materials and ideas for lesson studies.

World Association of Lesson Studies

In 2007 the World Association of Lesson Studies (WALS) was formed in Hong Kong. This organisation exists to share lesson studies and LS research and to promote LS practices around the world. Based in Singapore since 2011 its website (www.worldals.net) shares research and practice and its membership is now over 1,000 from over 40 different countries across all five continents. WALS sponsors an annual international conference each autumn in different parts of the world. Japan has also been active globally through its cultural development project Japan International Cooperation Agency (JICA). It supports the improvement of educational standards through LS in developing countries in East Asia, Africa, and Central and South America.

In addition, since 2012 LS has had its own international research journal: *The International Journal for Lesson and Learning Studies* (IJLLS) published by Emerald. IJLLS publishes articles specifically related to either LS or its close variant 'Learning Study' (which is particularly popular in Hong Kong and Sweden).

At the time of writing at least a handful of universities in the UK have built LS into their masters and initial teacher training programmes and the number of LS-based PhDs is burgeoning.

I will leave the final word in this first chapter to Professor Charles Desforges who kindly contributed the Foreword to this book, who first introduced me to the concept of research lessons in 2001 and who has remained a friend and guide ever since. Reflecting on why professional learning like LS is important and why it is important to carry out LS with colleagues from across the system, he had this to say:

> Much of what we [teachers] know and do is beyond our immediate consciousness, embedded in the taken for granted social constructions of particular classrooms or schools, our professional knowledge is almost beyond our description ... we need the informed opinion of professionals beyond our parish if we are to achieve transformation.
>
> (Desforges, 2004: 7)

7 A guide to this book

In Chapter 2 Haiyan Xu and David Pedder provide us with a definitive review of the research literature as it pertains to LS. Xu and Pedder's review is comprehensive, thoughtful and very discerning. It takes the reader subtly through a history of LS as evidenced by the literature, through the contemporary accounts of the spread of LS worldwide and onto the implications of these for further research in the future and the potential for LS to reveal more about how teachers learn.

Chapter 3 picks up the theme of leading LS. For many of us in the West this provides important challenges for two reasons. One is practical: our school timetables and organisation tend to make it difficult for teachers to be in one classroom at the same time. The other reason is deeper and that is that LS often unearths what Jim O'Shea, a headteacher who is interviewed in this chapter, calls 'unexpected outcomes' which can threaten leaders who lack the confidence to deal with the non-linearity of school development. Issues such as dealing with complexity, growing LS as a self-renewing process that improves learning and teaching, and leading LS across networks and systems of schools are discussed in interview with Jim and three other pioneers of LS in the UK: Sue Teague, Gill Jordan and Jean Lang. Their leadership insights are provided directly to the reader as they speak.

In Chapter 4 Annamari Ylonen and Brahm Norwich describe their study of how pupils and teachers benefited from using LS in a three-year research project exploring the ways LS helps teachers to understand how better to support the learning of pupils with learning difficulties and disabilities. They reveal how LS helps teachers to understand the reasons why particular pupils find learning difficult and how it also helps them find ways to support their learning as a result of this. It also goes on to suggest that because LS can provide deeply formative and diagnostic insights into pupils' learning which are strengthened by the fact that they are made in the learning context it should be developed as an assessment tool.

Chapter 5 focuses on how LS can help student teachers and their school-based mentors to learn how to learn how to teach. Wasyl Cajkler and Phil Wood report on their very practical research involving both trainees and school-based mentors as well as academic leads from the University of Leicester. This outlines LS's potential for helping trainee teachers more effectively to engage with the knowledge and experience of their mentors and of other teachers in their placement schools as they seek to enhance both their practice and their abilities to articulate and adjust their practice knowledge. The authors make a strong case for the use of LS in initial teacher education in this way.

In Chapter 6 Hiroyuki Kuno describes a process to which I believe we in the UK should aspire. He describes how, in Japan, the discipline of LS has allowed teachers, pupils and local system leaders such as 'research schools' and universities to grow the country's national curriculum which is founded not upon what is foremost in the minds of ministers at the time but on an ever-evolving understanding of how children have been found most effectively to learn, through the constant enquiry into learning, teaching and curriculum that happens in Japan's schools each year through their lesson studies.

Finally, in Chapter 7, David Pedder draws together some key themes from this book as a whole. He draws our attention to the need to dig deeper into the learning issues that are emerging from our lesson studies, to the opportunities that can be afforded by making more of the agency of pupils in LS. Yet he also points out the wider opportunities afforded by emerging organisations like teaching school alliances and the value many of them now place upon and gain from LS as a means of developing and transfering not only pedagogical practices but also the infectious enthusiasm with which most teachers embrace LS and all that it offers us for the future.

Notes

1 Pedagogical Content Knowledge (Shulman, 1986) refers to the knowledge of the content that it is necessary to have in order to teach that content. For example (Ball *et al*., 2008) contrast the content knowledge of how to use place value possessed by most people who use mathematics in the work place with knowledge a teacher needs to teach place value to a child – which involves not only knowing how to use place value in practice but also how it relates to the whole of the number system as well as what common misconceptions and aberrations children are prone to in relation to place value when learning about it.
2 The Camden Local Education Authority and University of Cambridge Lesson Study in Mathematics in Higher Order Teaching and Learning programme; the Edge Hill University Education Endowment Foundation Lesson Study programme; the DfE/CUREE Narrowing the Gap Study; the Barnet Primary Lesson Study Project.
3 The Camden New Curriculum Mathematics Lesson Study Programme (2013–15) is funded by the London Schools Excellence Fund and involves 25 primary and secondary schools in its first year, widening to as many as 90 in its second year. One of the hypotheses that it is exploring, originally reported in Dudley (2013), is that teacher talk in LS contexts can allow teachers to access each other's tacit professional knowledge stores and improve learning for pupils as a result.

References

Arnot, M., McIntyre, D., Pedder, D. and Reay, D. (2004). *Consultation in the Classroom: Developing Dialogue about Teaching and Learning*. London: Pearson Publishing.

Ball, D., Hoover-Thames, M. and Phelps, G. (2008). Content knowledge for teaching: what makes it special. *Journal of Teacher Education*, 59(5): 389–407.

Chen, X. (2011). Implications of Lesson Study for teacher professional development in China. Paper presented at the annual conference of the World Association of Lesson Study, Tokyo, December.

Chichibu, T. (2014). Reflections on lesson study in the UK, Japan and Kazakhstan. http://lessonstudy.co.uk/2014/01/toshiya-chichibu

Desforges, C.W. (2004). Collaboration: why bother? *Nexus*, 3: 6–7.

Dudley, P. (2003). *Planning, Conducting and Analysing Research Lessons: A Handbook for Practitioners*. Nottingham: NCSL.

Dudley, P. (2011). Lessons for learning: how teachers learn in contexts of Lesson Study. PhD thesis, University of Cambridge.

Dudley, P. (2012). Lesson Study development in England: from school networks to national policy. *International Journal of Lesson and Learning Studies*, 1(1): 85–100.

Dudley, P. (2013). Teacher learning in Lesson Study: What interaction-level discourse analysis revealed about how teachers utilised imagination, tacit knowledge of teaching and fresh evidence of pupils learning, to develop practice knowledge and so enhance their pupils' learning. *Teaching and Teacher Education*, 34: 107–21.

Dudley, P. (2014). *Lesson Study: A Handbook*. Cambridge: LSUK. http://lessonstudy.co.uk/lesson-study-a-handbook/

Erden, Z., Von Krogh, G. and Nonaka, I. (2008). The quality of group tacit knowledge. *The Journal of Strategic Information Systems*, 17(1), March: 4–18.

Gopesh A., Ward, P. and Tatikonda, M. (2010). Role of explicit and tacit knowledge in Six Sigma projects: An empirical examination of differential project success. *Journal of Operations Management*, 28(4), July: 303–15.

Hadfield, M., Jopling, M. and Emira, M. (2011). *Evaluation of the National Strategies' Primary Leading Teachers Programme*. Wolverhampton: University of Wolverhampton.

Hargreaves, D. (2012). *A Self Improving School System: Towards Maturity*. Nottingham: NCSL.

Hau, Y., Kim, B., Lee, H. and Kim, Y-G. (2013). The effects of individual motivations and social capital on employees' tacit and explicit knowledge sharing intentions. *International Journal of Information Management*, 33(2), April: 356–66.

Koskinen, L., Pihlanto, P. and Vanharanta, H. (2003). Tacit knowledge acquisition and sharing in a project work context. *International Journal of Project Management*, 21(4), May: 281–90.

Koskinen, K. and Vanharanta, H. (2002). The role of tacit knowledge in innovation processes of small technology companies. *International Journal of Production Economics*, 80(1), November: 57–64.

Lewis, C. (1998). A lesson is like a swiftly flowing river: how research lessons improve Japanese education. *American Educator*, Winter: 12–17 and 50–1.

McKinsey & Company (2007). *How the world's best-performing school systems come out on top*. London: McKinsey & Company.

Mercer, N. (2004). Sociocultural discourse analysis: analysing classroom talk as a social mode of thinking. *Journal of Applied Linguistics*, 1(2): 37–68.

Mourshed, M., Chijioke, C. and Barber, M. (2010). *How the world's most improved school systems keep getting better*. London: McKinsey & Company.

Pollard, A., Black-Hawkins, C., Cliff-Hodges, G., Dudley, P., James, M., Linklater, H., Swaffield, S., Swann, M., Turner, F., Warwick, P., Winterbottom, M. and Wolpert, A. (2014). *Reflective Teaching in Schools*. London: Bloomsbury.

Shulman, L. (1986). Those who understand knowledge growth in teaching. *Education Researcher*, 15(2): 4–14.

Stigler, J. and Hiebert, J. (1999). *The Teaching Gap*. New York: Free Press.

Vygotsky, L.S. (1986). *Thought and Language*. Massachusetts: Massachusetts Institute of Technology.

Wragg, E.C., Wikely, F., Wragg, E. and Haynes, G. (1996). *Teacher Appraisal Observed*. London: Routledge.

Chapter 2

Lesson Study

An international review of the research

Haiyan Xu and David Pedder

Introduction

Lesson Study (LS) is a classroom-based, lesson-specific and collaborative mode of teacher professional learning that has been practised in
Japan and China for decades (Chokshi and Fernandez 2005; Fernandez,
2002; Pang and Marton, 2003). LS has been used by teachers in Japan
since the early 1900s as a grassroots strategy for tackling problems
faced in classroom lessons by teachers and pupils (Ono and Ferreira,
2010). In China LS began to be promoted in schools in the 1950s by
the Ministry of Education as a way of developing the then large propor-
tion of untrained teachers in the country (China Ministry of Education,
1952). To date, in both Japan and China, LS has become a well-
established and widely used professional learning practice that is
deeply embedded in schools and at the local, regional and national
levels of their respective education systems (Fernandez, 2005; Tsui and
Wong, 2010).

However, LS had not been widely known outside China and Japan
until publication in 1999 of *The Teaching Gap: Best Ideas from the
World's Teachers for Improving Education in the Classroom* by Stigler
and Hiebert. The context of their research was the Trends in International
Mathematics and Science Study (TIMSS) in which large achievement
gaps in mathematics and science were identified between American
students and their counterparts from about half of the other 40 nations
taking part in the tests. Postulating whether the quality of teaching was
a significant cause of such differences, these researchers undertook
their research in order to compare videotaped mathematics lessons
conducted by teachers from three countries, the US, Germany and
Japan.

The study identified clear patterns of differences in mathematics
teaching in the three countries, especially between the US and Japan.

For example mathematics lessons in the US were characterised by teachers demonstrating specific mathematical procedures and students uncritically following these procedures and applying them to questions whether they understood the underlying maths or not. But in Japan, ranked in the top five in TIMSS, mathematics lessons were characterised by classroom tasks that encouraged student development of advanced mathematical thinking and experimentation with alternative mathematical solutions. The researchers Stigler and Hiebert, after their field investigations, attributed the high quality of mathematics teaching in Japan to a nationally adopted practice among its teachers that allows them to collaboratively develop professional knowledge, improve their teaching practice and gradually, and through joint efforts, change the overall culture of teaching. And that practice is Lesson Study.

On the basis of findings from their research Stigler and Hiebert recommended that any educational reform should be deemed ineffective if insufficient support was provided for teachers to effectively develop and share their teaching knowledge. They called for US policy makers and educators to promote collaborative work such as LS among their teachers to enable a transformation of teaching culture and successful implementation of educational reforms at the classroom level in the US.

Since the release of Stigler and Hiebert's book, LS has captured worldwide attention and, in a matter of a decade, spread to countries and regions including those in North America, Europe, Africa, the Middle East and other parts of Asia. One key explanation for its popularity is probably that in an international atmosphere of dissatisfaction and disappointment with traditional teacher professional development practices such as one-stop workshops, LS appears to offer more positive ways forward (Schwille *et al.*, 2007; Villegas-Reimers, 2003). LS procedures typically involve a group of three to seven teachers working collaboratively through cycles of planning, teaching/observing, evaluating and revising a lesson in order to develop improved ways of supporting pupils' learning. In this sense, lessons that are developed through LS processes can be understood as working hypotheses, developed together by teachers in LS teams, about how best to support pupils' learning in relation to a specific problem or issue their pupils encounter in their learning. Planning and evaluation meetings, together with the observed lesson itself, provide cycles through which the lesson (or working hypothesis) is critiqued and refined on the basis of observation evidence and the collective perspectives of the teachers involved.

In this way, LS brings together, within a shared and very clear set of procedures, opportunities for reflection, collaboration, research and experimentation that can contribute to professional learning and improvements in classroom practice. Through such procedures, teachers can undertake a more continuous, collaborative and practice-based approach to teacher learning – a mode of learning that has been identified by many researchers as effective for enhancing teachers' learning and classroom practice (e.g., Dudley, 2011a; Garet *et al.*, 2001; Pedder *et al.*, 2005; Pedder, 2006; Pedder and Opfer, 2013; Quicke, 2000; Schwille *et al.*, 2007; Villegas-Reimers, 2003).

Stigler and Hiebert's landmark study in 1999 makes a significant contribution to the international development of LS. Since publication of their book, research interest in LS has grown substantially, first in the USA and later to other major regions including Asia, Europe, Africa and the Middle East. In 2005, the World Association of Lesson Study was established in Hong Kong and today it has members from over 60 countries. Since 1999, research studies have been carried out in a variety of national, cultural, educational and institutional settings. It is timely then for us to stand back and take stock of how useful LS is as a strategy for enhancing the quality of professional learning and practice development. In this chapter we review research that has been carried out into LS since 1999.

We have included details of our literature search and review procedures in the appendix to this chapter for those interested in our methods. We turn now to review the findings from our review of LS research.

Findings from Lesson Study research

We found it convenient to report findings from LS research in relation to the following themes: growth and geographical spread of LS research, school settings and subject focus, sample characteristics and scale of LS research, variations and adaptations of LS, research focus and findings.

Growth and geographical spread of LS

We identified 67 articles published between 2002 and 2013. The first research paper on LS to be published was written by Fernandez, and appeared in 2002. There had been publications before this in the late 1990s but these tended to be introductory texts or conceptual

Table 2.1 Geographical distribution of LS articles included in the review

Continents	No. of articles	Countries
North America	34	USA (32), Canada (2)
Asia	23	Hong Kong (6), Singapore (4), China (3), Japan (2), Indonesia (2), Israel (1), Malaysia (1), Australia (1), Vietnam (1), Brunei (1), Turkey (1)
Europe	8	UK (5), Spain (1), Sweden (1), Ireland (1)
South Africa	2	South Africa (2)

discussions about the LS approach and its potential (Cohan and Honigsfeld, 2007).

Between 2002 and 2007 17 articles reporting empirical research into LS, and meeting our criteria of rigour, were published. Between 2008 and 2013 there was a more than three-fold increase to 50 articles reflecting the current growth in interest in LS. Alongside this numerical increase there has also been a wider spread of geographical contexts in which LS has been researched. Initially, there was a predominance of studies carried out in North America and Asia. More recently research interest in LS has spread to Europe and Africa.

Most research into LS continues to be conducted in Singapore, Hong Kong, China, Japan, UK and North America, in particular the USA, where about half the studies have been undertaken. Encouragingly, interest in LS is also growing in developing countries in Asia and Africa. According to Isoda *et al.* (2007) and Yuk (2011), LS has also been adopted in Cambodia, Egypt, Ghana, Honduras, Kenya, Laos, the Philippines, Thailand and Iran. Nevertheless, to our best knowledge, not all LS research in these countries have been identified in the international literature. Table 2.1 shows the geographic distribution of articles included in our review.

School settings and subject focus

It is clear from our review that LS has been used by teachers in formal educational settings from pre-school to university. The majority of research into LS has been carried out in primary school, secondary school and initial teacher education settings. In terms of subject focus, it tends to be mathematics and science teachers that are represented most in the reviewed studies. This pattern mirrors the findings from the survey conducted by Lim *et al.* (2011) with over 100 schools in

Singapore where more than half the number of LS teams in both primary and secondary schools focused on mathematics and science. This is also reflected in the USA (see Lewis, Perry and Friedkin, 2009). Indeed, in the USA it was through the work of mathematics and science teacher educators and researchers that LS was singled out for wide attention (Fernandez, 2002; Lewis *et al.*, 2006; Stigler and Hiebert, 1999). Our review also shows however that the spread and influence of LS has expanded to other disciplines such as ESL, literacy, the humanities, and business and economics.

Sample characteristics

Unsurprisingly the sample sizes in the research studies differ significantly, ranging from a small group of teachers to teachers from hundreds of schools. Apart from differences in size, the samples also differ in their constitution. We have identified four main kinds of samples and LS configuration in the reviewed research: a) department/school-based LS groups, b) cross-school LS groups, c) whole district LS networks, and d) course-based LS groups (as in the case of initial teacher education (ITE)). In addition, one study used large-scale samples that included teachers from over a hundred schools (Lim *et al.*, 2011). This indicates that while in some countries LS is being promoted by researchers and educators on a group-by-group basis (Holmqvist, 2011; Inoue, 2011; Lieberman, 2009) and also on a school-by-school basis (Sibbald, 2009; West-Olatunji *et al.*, 2008), some other countries are already trying to implement LS on a much more ambitious scale, for example as a district-wide practice as reported in the US (Fernandez, 2002; Perry and Lewis, 2009), and at a regional and provincial scale involving hundreds of schools as reported in Indonesia, Australia and Singapore (Saito *et al.*, 2006; White and Lim, 2008; Lim *et al.*, 2011). In a few countries and regions such as Singapore, Indonesia, Vietnam and Hong Kong, LS is promoted in schools and supported at the national level by Ministries of Education with resources and funding available to support educational reform on a national scale. Dudley (2007, 2011b) reported the spread of LS practice in the UK from the pilot stage of the Economic and Social Research Council (ESRC) and Teaching and Learning Research Programme (TLRP)-funded Learning How to Learn Project involving 14 schools to nationwide promotion and uptake by schools across England through inclusion of LS as part of the English Government's Primary National Strategies initiative.

Variations and adaptations of LS

As Stigler and Hiebert (1999) note, teaching is a cultural activity, and so local adaptations and variations of LS are only to be expected. Indeed, the practice of LS has developed a range of interesting variations. In Japan, for example, Saito (2012) has pointed out two broad types of LS approaches. One LS approach is used by national and regional educational authorities to disseminate pedagogical information such as the Open House Lesson Study (Dudley, 2007; Fernandez, 2002). A well-refined lesson that has been developed through several LS cycles is taught by a member of a LS team with a class of students in a large venue such as an auditorium or gymnasium. This public lesson is taught in the presence of an invited audience of other teachers, leaders and administrators. The size of the audience varies but can be as many as 1,000. Typically, a regional public lesson will attract an audience of about 100.

The other broad approach is much more local, private and school-based with teachers forming LS teams in subject departments or as part of a whole school professional learning strategy such as Lesson Study for the Learning Community (Saito, 2012; Saito *et al.*, 2012). In recent years, some scholars have been calling for collaboration between teachers and researchers in LS processes to maximise the benefits of LS (Fernandez, 2002, 2005; Lewis *et al.*, 2006; Oshima *et al.*, 2006). This has given rise to a new form of LS called Design Study (Oshima *et al.*, 2006) which is LS coupled with design research aimed at combining and integrating the research expertise of university researchers with the teaching expertise of school teachers in the LS process.

In a similar vein, LS has been developed in Hong Kong and Sweden (Holmqvist, 2011; Pang and Marton, 2003). Learning Study can be understood as LS combined with Variation Theory as a guiding principle for lesson planning and pedagogic design in the process of lesson development (Pang and Marton, 2003). The central tenet of Variation Theory is that learning entails a crucial process of discerning the critical and distinctive features of a phenomenon that one has not been able to discern before (Lo and Pong, 2006). Translated into a pedagogic principle, Variation Theory proposes that the task of a teacher in the classroom is to help learners to grasp most effectively those critical features of an object of learning.

To prepare a lesson in a LS group, teachers essentially do two things. First, they engage in in-depth analysis of the object of learning and identify its critical defining features and properties. Second, they investigate differences among learners in terms of their prior experiences and understandings in relation to the focal object of learning. And this enables them to identify variations in the learning needs of different groups of students prior to the lesson. This process of explicit and shared analysis of a) the critical features of a learning object and b) differences in the knowledge and understanding among a class of pupils serves as the basis for the LS group to plan a lesson. The distinctive value of incorporating Variation Theory in LS is so that planning, teaching and evaluating lessons and pupils' learning can be informed by an explicit theory of learning in relation to specific learning objects. LS provides teachers with a framework for evaluating and analysing variation in pupils' learning outcomes at the end of each lesson. Such a commitment is procedurally reflected in the use of pre- and post-tests as part of the LS process and in teachers' focused discussions and reflections around the critical features of the object of learning during planning and evaluation meetings. The incorporation of Variation Theory in LS processes reflects a commitment to building in a structured mechanism for analysing and tracing variations in pupil's progress and learning. A distinctive focus in teachers' analyses of pupils' test outcomes is on how different pupils vary in their test performance in relation to questions related to specific critical features of a learning object. Subsequent lessons are planned to address identified patterns of variations in a class of pupils' attained understandings in relation to the focal object of learning.

A number of other LS variations have been developed in China. The most well known variation in the international literature is Action Education (AE) (Gu and Wang, 2006), sometimes referred to as *Keli* (Huang and Bao, 2006). AE was developed and promoted in China in the context of the latest chapter of curriculum reform as a mechanism to support teachers in their classroom experimentation and implementation of new curriculum content and pedagogical principles (Paine and Fang, 2006). While sharing core features with typical procedures of LS such as collaborative lesson planning, observation and evaluation, AE highlights the importance of engaging external experts such as university researchers, curriculum developers and subject specialists in the working of the AE teams. External experts provide guidance in the interpretation of new curriculum ideas. A key departure of AE from LS is its explicit orientation to develop the learning and practice of a focus teacher while at the same time sustaining commitment to the learning and practice development of the entire AE team.

This orientation is reflected in aspects of its procedures. For example, after the team has formed and met initially to discuss and agree the theme and topic of their lesson study, a focus teacher is usually chosen to devise a detailed lesson plan on his/her own. The same teacher then teaches the lesson with a class for other members of the team to observe. After observation, collaborative evaluation of the lesson may lead to identification of positive and/or negative aspects of pupils' engagement and performance in the lesson and factors that may have caused barriers to pupils' learning. Typical factors may include problems with aspects of the lesson itself such as the design of the lesson, the appropriateness of activities used, the effectiveness of teaching methods adopted, and the ways certain activities were carried out by the focus teacher. The focus teacher then responds to the feedback from the other members of the AE team, and in the light if this, revises the lesson and teaches it a second time. This procedure can be repeated until the team is confident that their developed lesson reflects and embodies the principles recommended by the new curriculum standards and achieves the aim of effectively supporting pupil learning. AE procedures clearly differ from conventional LS in relation to the much clearer emphasis of AE on the learning and practice development of an individual focus teacher.

These identified variations of LS echo the observation of White and Lim (2008: 916) that 'the term Lesson Study has become an umbrella term for a variety of adaptations or global responses'. Apart from these distinctive forms of LS variations, our review also identifies various practical adaptations and modifications to LS procedures in face of specific needs and constraints in local institutional settings. These adaptations occur when LS approaches are used to support ITE and in-service teacher development. In ITE settings, for example, due to student teachers' lack of direct classroom experience, ITE course lecturers often assign student teachers a study focus or provide them with topics to choose instead of asking them to identify a LS focus independently (Chassels and Melville, 2009; Marble, 2007; Parks, 2008). A second adaptation in ITE occurs when trainees cannot be allocated with a class of their own. In such cases peer teaching or micro-teaching are incorporated as a substitute for actual classroom teaching (Carrier, 2011; Fernández, 2010; Fernández and Robinson, 2006; Ricks, 2011; White and Lim, 2008).

In both ITE and in-service teacher development settings, two other practical adaptations have been identified and they relate to the evaluation steps of the LS process. One is that the number of plan-teach/observe-evaluate procedures conducted within one LS cycle varies from one to as many as necessary depending on the local conditions in which LS is being undertaken (Chassels and Melville, 2009; Cohan and Honigsfeld, 2007; Dotger, 2011; Lim *et al.*, 2011; Parks 2008; White and Lim, 2008). The other is that, in cases of logistic and administrative difficulties such as lack of cover to free teachers up to observe lessons, observation of live classrooms are sometimes replaced by observation of recorded lesson videos (Cohan and Honigsfeld, 2007; Inoue, 2011; Lieberman, 2009; White and Lim, 2008). And these adaptations do not appear to have harmed the overall reported usefulness of LS for enhancing teacher and pupil learning outcomes. Indeed, as Lewis *et al.* (2006: 5) argue, a good innovation should allow scope for developing 'a more thoughtful and flexible approach' in application.

Perhaps LS has spread so quickly across continents, countries and school and classroom settings because it provides practical contexts that allow teachers to learn and enhance their practice directly in the contexts at the heart of their professional work – classroom lessons. Another reason for the extraordinary spread of LS might be the clarity and simplicity of the procedures on the one hand and the scope and flexibility in these procedures that allow teachers and teacher educators to adapt the ways they work together. It is this versatility of LS that allows teachers to learn and change together in flexible, locally adapted, relevant and practical ways.

Research focus and findings

We identified four main categories of research into LS according to research focus and findings. The first category consists of 49 articles (73 per cent of all reviewed articles) focused on the benefits and constraints that influence LS in different contexts. The second category consists of nine articles (14 per cent of all reviewed articles) focused on how LS is used by teachers and teacher educators as a method to investigate specific aspects of teaching and learning. These articles tend to have a dual focus, with the primary and explicit focus on the specific aspect of teaching and learning under investigation, such as 'use of manipulatives in mathematics classrooms and its influence on pupil learning', and a second and sometimes implied focus on the benefits of LS for teacher learning and practice development. The third category consists of five articles (7 per cent of all reviewed articles) which go further into learning processes and aim at helping us understand more about how LS contributes to enhanced quality of professional learning and classroom practice. The fourth category consists of four articles (6 per cent of all reviewed articles) that focus on contextual factors and identify factors that influence how successfully LS can be implemented and sustained. We found it interesting that so much research has been concerned with questions of benefits and implementation challenges and so little research with questions of how teachers learn and develop practice through participation in LS. Table 2.2 summarises the range of research focus together with the geographic locations of the research studies listed.

In the rest of the section, we elaborate on the focus for each of our four categories before summarising the main findings.

1. Benefits and constraints in the use of LS

Researchers in this group were generally interested in testing the benefits and usefulness of LS in a particular local context and finding out the potential constraints and challenges in its implementation. The majority of the studies reported positive benefits derived from LS related to:

- Teacher collaboration and development of a professional learning community
- Development of professional knowledge, practice and professionalism
- More explicit focus on pupil learning
- Improved quality of classroom teaching and learning

TEACHER COLLABORATION AND DEVELOPMENT OF A PROFESSIONAL LEARNING COMMUNITY

As Puchner and Taylor summarise it, 'collaboration among teachers has been identified as one of the most important features of a school culture that fosters professional development, teacher satisfaction, teacher effectiveness and student achievement within a school' (2006: 924). Twenty-one studies in this category highlighted the benefits of teacher collaboration through LS with evidence from the testimonies of teachers and the observation records of researchers (Kotelawala, 2012). These studies reported an increase in teachers' collegiality, joint decision making, and joint ownership and responsibility for teaching leading to

Table 2.2 LS research focus and geographic location

Research focus	No. of articles	Geographical locations
Benefits (and constraints) of LS approach on TPD in local contexts	49	USA (23), Hong Kong (5), China (3), South Africa (2), Indonesia (2), Japan (1), Singapore (3), Brunei (1), Malaysia (1), Canada (2), UK (3), Spain (1), Sweden (1), Turkey (1)
Using LS to investigate specific aspects of teaching and learning	9	
• teaching consensus building strategy		USA (1)
• use of manipulatives in maths class		USA (1)
• teaching informal inferential reasoning		Ireland (1)
• teachers' technological pedagogical content knowledge		USA (1)
• preservice teachers' reflective thinking		USA (1)
• preservice teachers' academic, school and pedagogical mathematics		USA (1)
• teaching standards		Australia (1)
• accountability testing		USA (1)
• pedagogy development for students with moderate learning difficulties (MLD)		UK (1)
How teachers learn through LS	5	
• collaborative cognitive processes		Israel (1)
• process reflection		USA (1)
• expansive learning		HK (1)
• knowledge synthesising, tension negotiating, and belief and practice transforming		USA (1)
• language mediation of teachers' learning		UK (1)
Other themes	4	
• conditions and factors that support LS implementation and sustainability		USA (1), Singapore (1), Vietnam (1)
• importance of teacher-researcher collaboration in LS		Japan (1)

the cultivation of professional learning communities (Andrew, 2011; Cohan and Honigsfeld, 2007; Fernández and Robinson, 2006; Hunter and Back, 2011; Lawrence and Chong, 2010; Parks, 2009; Sims and Walsh, 2009). Participants in LS benefit from mutual sharing of knowledge and resources about teaching and learning (Davies and Dunnill, 2008; Dudley, 2013; Lewis, Perry and Hurd, 2009; Pang, 2006; Sibbald, 2009); focused and in-depth discussions about classroom issues (Roback *et al.*, 2006; Rock and Wilson, 2005); regular peer observation of each other's practice (Gu and Wang, 2006; Gurl, 2011; Yang, 2009); constructive peer feedback on each other's teaching practice (Cheng and Yee, 2012; Gu and Wang, 2006; Huang and Bao, 2006; Rock and Wilson, 2005); and the sharing of multiple perspectives on how to foster successful pupil learning in classrooms (Roback *et al.*, 2006; Sibbald, 2009).

DEVELOPMENT OF TEACHER KNOWLEDGE, PRACTICE AND PROFESSIONALISM

Nineteen studies in this category reported that LS helped teachers to develop professional knowledge, professional practice and an enhanced sense of professionalism (Dudley, 2013; Lee, 2008, Marble, 2007; Ono *et al.*, 2011; Rock and Wilson, 2005). With a range of evidence from teacher interviews, researcher observations, and teachers' collaborative talk, researchers have reported significant improvement in teachers' knowledge and skills such as gains in their subject content knowledge (Dudley, 2011a, 2013; Fernandez, 2005, Lewis, 2009; Yang, 2009); pedagogical knowledge (Dudley, 2011a, 2013; Fernandez, 2005; Lewis, Perry and Hurd, 2009; Marble, 2007); knowledge about pupils (Dudley, 2011a, 2013; Fernandez, 2005; Lee, 2008; Lewis, 2009; Marble, 2007); knowledge about technology for teaching (Meng and Sam, 2011); and in addition, teacher's pedagogical content knowledge (Dudley, 2011a, 2013; Fernandez, 2005; Lawrence and Chong, 2010; Lewis, 2009; Lewis, Perry and Hurd, 2009; Sibbald, 2009). In sum, a growing body of research evidence suggests that LS supports growth in the highly contextualised forms of knowledge that are directly relevant to and find their use and application in teachers' classroom practice. Such knowledge is also what student teachers in ITE settings tend to lack, however, where LS activities are used to structure school placements and are expected to acquire through their LS activities during school placements (Marble, 2006, 2007). Research by members of the Lesson Study Research Group at the University of Leicester School of Education, published after this review was undertaken, is developing important insights into the use of LS in ITE settings. See especially Cajkler *et al*. (2013) and Chapter 5 of this volume by Cajkler and Wood.

Furthermore, researchers report that participation in LS is helping teachers to develop an inquiry stance and become more critically reflective about their own practice (Andrew, 2011; Fernandez, 2005; Ricks, 2011). The cyclical plan-teach/observe-evaluate procedures of LS offer a kind of 'reflective immediacy' (Shulman, 2003 as cited in Fernandez, 2005: 283) that enables teachers to experience the outcomes of their reflective actions. This practical usefulness of LS encourages teachers to go on with further actions of reflection and practice refinement (Fernandez, 2005; Gu and Wang, 2006; Lewis, Perry and Hurd, 2009). Therefore LS is considered useful for supporting development of teachers as reflective practitioners who have the capacity to conduct teacher-initiated and teacher-led practice improvement (Fernandez, 2005).

In addition, researchers have reported that LS is helpful for changing teachers' attitudes and beliefs about teaching as a profession (Pella, 2011; Sibbald, 2009). Peer and collegial support among teachers in LS collaborations contribute to improvement in teachers' confidence in experimenting with new teaching ideas (Meng and Sam, 2011; Norwich and Ylonen, 2013; Rock and Wilson, 2005; Sibbald, 2009); their self-efficacy in making a positive impact on pupil learning through their teaching (Chong and Kong, 2012; Lawrence and Chong, 2010; Puchner and Taylor, 2006; Sibbald, 2009); and hence their sense of self as a teacher whose work is significant and meaningful (Cohan and Honigsfeld, 2007; Sibbald, 2009).

MORE EXPLICIT FOCUS ON PUPIL LEARNING

The primary concern of LS is to develop lessons, through carefully planned classroom strategies, that can better facilitate pupil learning (Dudley, 2003; Fernandez, 2005). Twenty-one studies used a range of evidence from excerpts of teachers' discussions and interactions during collaborative planning and evaluation meetings, observation records of research lessons, and teachers' testimonies to show that LS participation helps in-service teachers or student teachers to shift their focus from teaching to learning (Norwich and Ylonen, 2013; Pang, 2006; Perry and Lewis, 2009) and develop greater awareness and deeper insights about learners and their needs (Andrew, 2011; Chassels and Melville, 2009; Davies and Dunnill, 2008; Lee, 2008; Pang, 2006; Roback *et al.*, 2006; Rock and Wilson, 2005). For example the teachers or student teachers in these studies became more aware of and responsive to pupils' prior knowledge (Dotger, 2011; Lee, 2008) and more deliberately analytic about the learning goals of a lesson in relation to what their pupils already know (Holmqvist, 2011; Holmqvist *et al.*, 2012; Lawrence and Chong, 2010; Sims and Walsh, 2009; Yuk, 2011).

Teachers claimed to deepen their understandings of how and what pupils learn through closely observing selected pupils as they participate in lessons and through discussing together what they have observed and what they have understood through their observations. Dudley (2003) established the importance for teachers' learning and practice development of identifying case pupils and observing their participation closely during lessons. In introducing LS into the UK Dudley's focus on case pupils represents an important and distinctive development of LS procedures (Dudley, 2011a, 2013). Other researchers have also reported that analysing and reflecting on case pupil participation in lessons is a powerful means of enhancing teachers' planning, conduct and evaluation of lessons (e.g., Norwich and Ylonen, 2013).

Teachers working in LS contexts reported that through the insights they were developing about their pupils' learning, they were developing a greater responsiveness to their pupils' learning needs by aligning their teaching more closely to their pupils' knowledge and understandings, thus creating more favourable conditions for learning (Fernández, 2010; Lee, 2008; Marble, 2006). Researchers also reported that teachers become better at anticipating pupils' learning difficulties and formulating strategies for helping pupils master difficult elements of the curriculum (Budak, 2012; Gao and Ko, 2009; Hart, 2009; Yang, 2009). A further development in taking fuller advantage of pupil's insights and perspectives might be to involve pupils directly in the planning and evaluation of lessons.

IMPROVED QUALITY OF CLASSROOM TEACHING AND PUPIL LEARNING

Another frequently reported benefit of LS is that it enhances the quality of classroom teaching in support of improvements in the quality of pupil learning. Twenty-two studies provided a range of evidence including testimonies from teachers, observational records, and analysis of lesson videos to support claims about improvements in the quality of classroom teaching and learning as a result of LS participation (Fernandez, 2005; Gao and Ko, 2009; Huang and Bao, 2006; Lawrence and Chong, 2010; Lewis, 2009; Marble, 2007; Matoba *et al.*, 2007; Ono and Ferreira, 2010; Robinson and Leikin, 2012; Rock and Wilson, 2005; Sims and Walsh, 2009).

These studies identified three main processes through which LS makes a difference to the quality of classroom practice: first, through developing teachers' professional knowledge and beliefs which then leads to improvement in the kinds of classroom strategies they develop for supporting enhanced pupil learning (Fernandez, 2005; Huang and Bao, 2006; Lewis, 2009; Sibbald, 2009; Ylonen and Norwich, 2012); second, through developing teachers' personal qualities and dispositions, such as their sense of self-efficacy and professional identity, which motivate them to assume more responsibilities for pupil learning (Chong and Kong, 2012; Lewis, Perry and Hurd, 2009; Sibbald, 2009); and third, through changing the norms and dynamics that shape teachers' participation in communities of practice towards development of safe and trustworthy environments in which teachers can share knowledge and resources and experiment with new ideas (Lewis, Perry and Hurd, 2009; Lieberman, 2009).

This group of studies developed three main types of evidence to reflect improvement in pupil learning. One type of evidence was developed from classroom observations of pupil engagement and performance during lessons. Claims to improvements in pupils' learning are based on comparisons between the classroom performance of pupils at one stage of a cycle with their performance at another later stage of a cycle (Lewis, Perry and Hurd, 2009; Norwich and Ylonen, 2013; Robinson and Leikin, 2012; Rock and Wilson, 2005). A second type of evidence, which is prevalent in LS papers, is developed through tests administered to pupils before and after a research lesson to find out whether improvements in their knowledge or understanding about a particular learning objective have been achieved (Andrew, 2011). The third type of evidence is established on the basis of changes in pupils' academic attainments reflected in standardised tests. This type of evidence is used to support claims about the long-term impact of using LS as a routine aspect of teacher or school practice (Gu and Wang, 2006; Matoba *et al.*, 2007; Saito *et al.*, 2012).

CONSTRAINTS AND CHALLENGES

A number of important practical constraints and challenges associated with the implementation of LS have been identified by researchers (Demir *et al.*, 2012; Fernandez, 2002, 2005; Fernandez *et al.*, 2003; Norwich and Ylonen, 2013). The most frequently mentioned constraints are the lack of time for teachers to engage in LS activities (Chassels and Melville, 2009; Fernandez, 2002; Lee, 2008; Norwich and Ylonen, 2013), the extra stress or demand put on teachers to interrogate and refine their practice (Lee, 2008), and lack of strong leadership support to create favourable conditions for teachers to implement and sustain LS practice (Meng and Sam, 2011; Saito *et al.*, 2006; Saito *et al.*, 2008; Ylonen and Norwich, 2012).

Another significant challenge relates to the often entrenched nature of current practice and fossilisation of classroom and school cultures. These can act as a brake on innovative developments in learning and practice development through LS (Demir *et al.*, 2012; Fernandez *et al.*, 2003; Ono *et al.*, 2011; Ono and Ferreira, 2010; Saito *et al.*, 2006; Saito *et al.*, 2008; Saito *et al.*, 2012). Tensions or conflicts can occur when processes aimed at supporting changes in the way teachers work are introduced. For example fear and suspicion in a culture of surveillance, performance audit and performance-related pay can hamper efforts to shift from a private, individualistic and sometimes competitive way of working towards a collaborative orientation based on interdependence and a mutual concern among teachers for one another's learning and practice development as a collective shared enterprise (Chassels and Melville, 2009; Puchner and Taylor, 2006). On the other hand, cultural tendencies that lead to conflict avoidance and decisions to duck the critical questions obstruct genuinely constructive forms of collaboration (Lewis, Perry and Hurd, 2009; Rock and Wilson, 2005). Furthermore, school and classroom cultures that emphasise a narrowly construed performance orientation and managerialist approach centred on pupil performance data, target setting and monitoring at the expense of broader questions of sustained learning and the conditions that promote it at all levels of the school organisation can prevent teachers from taking risks. In order to learn, teachers need to have the confidence (and permission) to share what they are struggling with in their practice as well as what they are confidently doing well. In other words they need to be free to face up to their weaknesses as well as their strengths – the building blocks of professional learning and practice development in support of pupil learning in contexts of LS (Fernandez *et al.*, 2003;

Ono and Ferreira, 2010; Ono *et al.*, 2011; Saito *et al.*, 2006; Saito *et al.*, 2008; Saito *et al.*, 2012).

2. Using LS in contexts of CPD and ITE

This category consists of nine research studies that were carried out to investigate specific aspects of classroom teaching and learning in continuing professional development (CPD) or ITE contexts. Three out of the nine studies explored the use of specific pedagogical strategies in classroom lessons and their influence on pupil learning (Inoue, 2011; Leavy, 2010; Puchner *et al.*, 2008). Two of the nine studies were conducted by teacher educators in ITE settings to investigate developments in their trainees' reflective thinking skills and their confidence about their mathematics knowledge (Jansen and Spitzer, 2009; Plummer and Peterson, 2009). Four studies investigated the application of LS in the classroom implementation of specific aspects of a policy reform (Yarema, 2010), development of classroom teaching strategies for tackling a particular focal issue (Kriewaldt, 2012; Ylonen and Norwich, 2012), and assessment of a certain aspect of teachers' knowledge or skills (Groth *et al.*, 2009) respectively.

3. Processes through which teachers learn in LS contexts

Disappointingly, we identified only five studies that have investigated the processes through which LS enables teachers to learn (Dudley, 2013; Pella, 2011; Ricks, 2011; Robinson and Leikin, 2012; Tsui and Law, 2007). Two studies explain how LS helps teachers to establish the kinds of thinking processes that are conducive for reflective practice and learning (Ricks, 2011; Robinson and Leikin, 2012). Ricks (2011) proposed, on the basis of evidence from teachers' collaborative meetings, that the procedures of LS create opportunities for teachers to learn through processes of collective reflection. According to his study, it is through a series of reflections during the lesson planning, teaching, observation and evaluation phases of a LS cycle that teachers develop new knowledge, understandings and beliefs about classroom teaching and pupil learning. Robinson and Leikin (2012) reported that participation in LS raises teachers' awareness of a particular issue and prompts them to share ideas and develop new understandings.

Another two studies each looked at processes of teachers' individual learning in interaction with others in communities of practice

(Pella 2011; Tsui and Law 2007). Pella (2011) describes a cross-community learning process with a focus on the challenges for teachers of having to renegotiate and transform perceptions and beliefs when they cross community boundaries and work with new teams and groups of teachers. Pella (2011) reported that learning is prompted by the ensuing cognitive dissonance and conceptual tensions or disequilibrium. Also from a cross-boundary perspective, Tsui and Law (2007) illustrate how a LS component of an initial teacher education programme involved student teachers, university lecturers and school mentors learning together by stepping across the traditional boundaries of their respective institutions in ways that promoted not only the learning of the student teachers but also that of university lecturers and school mentors.

Dudley's (2013) study, on the other hand, points our attention to a new facet of learning processes in LS contexts – the important interactive and discursive processes that mediate and support teachers' learning in collaboration. Drawing on socio-cultural theory and on Mercer's categories for distinguishing between different kinds of talk (Mercer, 1995, 2000), Dudley's research represents an important breakthrough in understanding the talk-mediation of teachers' learning. His study demonstrated the importance of exploratory talk in teachers' collaborative planning and evaluation meetings. A further important insight developed through Dudley's work is the importance of simulation and imaginative enactment as a planning strategy and as a means used by teachers in collaborative settings for representing tacit kinds of knowledge.

Although small in number, this group of studies has made an interesting start to the essential work of describing and explaining how learning takes place in LS processes. Nevertheless, there remains a great deal of further research and conceptual work to do before we arrive at a well-developed explanatory theory of teachers' and students' learning in LS contexts.

4. Conditions and factors that support successful and sustained implementation of LS

Three research studies investigated larger-scale LS practice and developed findings about factors and conditions that are important for successful and sustained implementation of LS. One study, conducted by Lim *et al.* (2011) involved working with 109 primary and secondary schools in Singapore that had implemented or experimented with LS. Through a survey questionnaire administered to school leaders, LS team leaders and teachers, the study identified five critical conditions, four of which are related to support from school leadership. Teachers reported that when school leaders are convinced about LS, they will create favourable school conditions and mobilise resources to enable successful conduct of LS. The survey also found that it is crucial to have teacher leaders who are prepared to take the initiative and drive forward LS activities (Lim *et al.*, 2011).

Another study was conducted by Perry and Lewis (2009) in the US about a teacher-initiated district-wide LS project that lasted for over four years. The researchers in this study identified a number of key factors that made the district-wide LS network successful and sustainable. One overall success factor is that initiators of this network maintained a flexible and pragmatic approach to promoting LS and were able to respond quickly to teachers' needs and make timely adaptations or adjustments to support teacher learning.

Saito *et al.* (2012) reported a school reform project carried out in the Vietnamese province of Bac Giang where a LS variation called Lesson Study for Learning Community was being developed experimentally in schools. Through their study, they found that in Bac Giang LS is successfully sustained in schools where teachers are convinced of its effectiveness, where there is strong leadership support, and where the schools themselves have a strong desire to maintain a reputation as a school with a well developed learning-orientation.

Although the three studies were conducted in different countries with different cultural characteristics, one consensus seems to be that in order to sustain LS practice in schools and classrooms, well developed systems of leadership and organisational support are necessary. Examples of such systems of leadership and organisational support are an explicit commitment among senior leadership teams to classroom-based and collaborative modes of teacher learning such as LS and its variants through, for example the allocation of financial resources to the provision of cover so that teachers are freed up to plan and evaluate lessons together and observe one another's lessons. Systems for recording and enabling access to excellent practice ideas and resources developed through teachers working together in LS teams not only support the dissemination and adaptation of innovative lessons in a range of classroom contexts, but also serve to validate excellent practice and the teachers involved in developing it.

Critical discussion of Lesson Study research

We identified a number of weaknesses in the reviewed research which we would like to discuss here. The majority of studies we reviewed neglected to address the question of processes through which the impact of LS on teacher learning and student outcomes is achieved. Indeed, only nine studies developed a theorised interest in teachers' learning processes and even in these articles the theoretical accounts were often vague. One problem is that researchers tend to be insufficiently clear about how a particular theoretical framework explains how particular aspects of the LS process influence learning. Another problem with LS research is the tendency to use theory to amplify social processes of learning at the expense of attending properly to individual learning processes (e.g., Salomon and Perkins, 1998). A number of researchers adopt situated learning theory to explain learning in LS contexts. They tend to highlight the role of teachers' communities of practice in shaping what teachers learn and do (Dotger, 2011; Lieberman, 2009; Oshima *et al.*, 2006; Parks, 2008; Pella, 2011; Robinson and Leikin, 2012; Sibbald, 2009; Tsui and Law, 2007). However, a typical feature of such research is that the active role of individual teachers in building their own knowledge is underplayed. Thus, it is often difficult to make explicit what individual teachers have learned (Edwards, 2005). In LS research there is still an absence of the kinds of theoretical work necessary for explaining how and why teachers learn both collectively and individually in LS contexts, and how features of LS procedures and contexts support and contribute to the individual and collective learning of teachers in LS. An exception to this trend is the explicitly theorised work of Dudley (2011a, 2013) who adopted a socio-cultural theoretical framework in his research into the language mediation of teachers' learning and practice development in LS contexts.

Another area of neglect lies in the kinds of evidence that researchers use to support their claims and conclusions. The majority of studies tend to rely on teachers' accounts of their perspectives elicited through interviews to establish their claims. These are very useful kinds of evidence, as it is the teachers who are directly involved in the LS processes and their perspectives are likely to contain useful insights into the conditions, processes and influences of LS on their practice and learning. However, there are only a small number of studies that explore how teacher's learning is achieved through their use of different kinds of talk and language, and these studies, with the notable exception of Dudley (2011a, 2013), tend to treat teachers' talk descriptively rather than as an important mediator of teachers' learning processes and outcomes (Fernandez, 2005; Oshima *et al.*, 2006; Ricks, 2011). Detailed and well theorised investigation into the ways teachers talk during their participation in LS and, further, whether certain kinds of talk among teachers are more effective than others in enabling teachers' learning and practice change in LS is, we feel, an important area for future research.

In almost all the studies, there was a lack of attention to important questions related to the micropolitical dimensions of teachers' collaborative work in LS contexts, such as the building of trust, establishing norms of collegiality characterised by the sharing and exchange of resources and ideas, and the resolution of conflict. Several studies have reported that collaboration in LS can be complex and 'messy' (Adamson and Walker, 2011; Chassels and Melville, 2009; Lewis, Perry and Hurd, 2009; Puchner and Taylor, 2006; Rock and Wilson, 2005). Genuine collaboration that is conducive to learning can be compromised because of conflict among teachers in the LS group (Puchner and Taylor, 2006), or conversely because of a deliberate avoidance of conflicts among teachers that leads to polite rather than critically constructive interaction (Lewis, Perry and Hurd, 2009; Rock and Wilson, 2005). Collaboration can also take the form of 'contrived collegiality' (Hargreaves, 1994 as cited in Adamson and Walker, 2011: 29) where there is superficial unanimity in the group but no generation of meaningful, critically constructive learning. But we found very little research apart from Adamson and Walker's study that has investigated micropolitical factors that influence teachers' collective learning and work in LS contexts. More studies are needed to help us further our understandings about micropolitical influences on LS processes and outcomes in different contexts.

Conclusion

So far our review of the research literature has shown that the influence of LS has spread across Asia, Europe, North America, Africa and the Middle East. The usefulness of LS in promoting teacher professional learning and practice development has been explored at different levels of education systems in different countries from early childhood to higher education contexts, and in contexts of in-service teacher professional development and initial teacher education. Most of the research carried out into LS has adopted a small-scale, qualitative, exploratory and inductive mode of inquiry that has helped researchers to study in-depth a range of variations of LS adapted for use in different local contexts. The majority of research studies have reported positive benefits derived from LS for teachers' learning and the quality of classroom teaching and learning. Evidence used to support these claims is developed from a range of data sources such as teacher testimonies from interviews or reflective journals, researcher field observations, observation and analysis of research lessons, and analysis of teacher collaborative meetings. Evidence used to support claims in pupil learning was mainly based on classroom observations about pupils' engagement and achievements in research lessons and, in a few cases, comparisons of students' performance in tests such as the pre- and post-tests in Learning Study and other standardised tests organised by educational authorities. In addition, the research literature has highlighted a few contextual factors and conditions that contribute to the success and sustainability of LS implementation, most notably strong leadership support. These research findings are significant in advancing our understandings about LS.

Appendix I The literature search and review process

We carried out a comprehensive literature search of the British Education Index (BEI), the Education Resources Information Center (ERIC) and the Australian Education Index (AUEI) databases using the search term 'lesson study'. We included peer-reviewed journal articles but excluded non peer-reviewed reports and conference papers. Our search generated a list of 141 articles in total, spanning the years 1999 to 2013. We then went through a screening process to select studies for this review. The first step involved reading through the abstracts of these papers to decide their relevance, a judgment based on whether or not LS was addressed as the main research issue. The second step involved reading the articles selected from the first round to ensure that we included only the most rigorous research in our review. We came to decisions about whether to include or exclude an article on the basis of whether the article included: i) conceptual discussion of how LS contributes to teachers' learning and/or development of classroom practice; ii) an explicit account of research design, particularly sample details and the methods and procedures for collecting and analysing data; and iii) a clear presentation of findings and conclusions based on the data. In the end, a total of 67 articles were included in this review. Our review was shaped by a concern to find out if, how and what teachers learn through working together in LS contexts. We were also interested in finding out how LS helps teachers develop their classroom practice in ways that help their pupils improve their learning. In relation to this main aim, we were also interested in the balance between the application of LS in initial teacher education and continuing professional learning settings. Furthermore, we were interested in how learning and professional development had been theorised in the reviewed studies.

As a routine part of our review procedures, we recorded the aims, objectives and research questions of the reviewed studies together with the characteristics of the teachers participating in any particular research study and the national and institutional context in which the research was carried out. We also recorded the research strategies and approaches used by the researchers whose work we reviewed.

Appendix 2 Methodology and research methods adopted in the studies

Sixty-two out of the 67 studies included in our review adopted small-scale qualitative research approaches. Almost all of these adopted a case study design. This preponderance of small-scale qualitative case study research that has been adopted by the majority of LS research teams has allowed for the development of useful descriptive findings about contextual variation in the ways different groups of teachers have used and adapted LS procedures to particular local contexts and needs.

A small number of research investigations have incorporated survey questionnaires, but these questionnaires were mainly employed to either collect information on the status of LS practice in schools, such as the scale and variation of participation, or to analyse patterns of teachers' perceptions about the benefits of participation in LS (Fernández and Robinson, 2006; Gu and Wang, 2006; Lim et al., 2011; Matoba et al., 2007).

Given the still small number of research studies that have been published, and the variations in ways that LS has been realised in practice in different contexts, we would argue that further qualitative, exploratory, open-ended and inductive research into LS is needed if we are to establish a broad base of contextualised understandings about the potential benefits of LS and the kinds of processes that improve and optimise the quality of teachers' and pupils' learning opportunities when working together in LS contexts. We agree with Lewis *et al.* (2006) when they argue that building up case-based records of contextualised understandings of LS and local variations is a necessary prior stage before subjecting the effectiveness of LS to summative test.

References

Adamson, B. and Walker E. (2011). Messy collaboration: learning from a learning study. *Teaching and Teacher Education*, 27(1): 29–36.

Andrew, V.A. (2011). Using Learning Study to improve the teaching and learning of accounting in a school in Brunei Darussalam. *International Journal for Lesson and Learning Studies*, 1(1): 23–40.

Budak, A. (2012). Mathematics teachers' engaging in a lesson study at virtual settings. *Educational Research and Reviews*, 7(15): 338–43.

Cajkler, W., Wood, P., Norton J. and Pedder, D. (2013). Lesson Study: towards a collaborative approach to learning in Initial Teacher Education? *Cambridge Journal of Education*, 43(4): 537–54.

Carrier, S.J. (2011). Implementing and integrating effective teaching strategies including features of Lesson Study in an elementary science methods course. *The Teacher Educator*, 46(2): 145–60.

Chassels, C. and Melville, W. (2009). Collaborative, reflective and iterative Japanese lesson study in an Initial Teacher Education Program: benefits and challenges. *Canadian Journal of Education*, 32(4): 734–63.

Cheng, L.P. and Yee, L.P. (2012). A Singapore case of Lesson Study. *The Mathematics Educator*, 21(2): 34–57.

Chokshi, S. and Fernandez, C. (2005). Reaping the systemic benefits of lesson study. *Phi Delta Kappan*, 86(9): 674–80.

Chong, A.H. and Kong, C.A. (2012). Teacher collaborative learning and teacher self-efficacy: The case of Lesson Study. *The Journal of Experimental Education*, 80(3): 263–83.

Cohan, A. and Honigsfeld, A. (2007). Incorporating 'Lesson Study' in Teacher Preparation. *The Educational Forum*, 71(1): 81–92.

Davies, P. and Dunnill, R. (2008). Learning Study as a model of collaborative practice in initial teacher education. *Journal of Education for Teaching*, 34(1): 3–16.

Demir, K., Sutton-Brown, C. and Czerniak, C. (2012). Constraints to Changing Pedagogical Practices in Higher Education: An example from Japanese lesson study. *International Journal of Science Education*, 34(11): 1709–39.

Dotger, S. (2011). Exploring and developing graduate teaching assistants' pedagogies via lesson study. *Teaching in Higher Education*, 16(2): 157–69.

Dudley, P. (2003). Using research lessons to improve pupil learning. Paper presented at the annual conference of the Association of South American English medium International Schools, Santiago, Chile, August 2003.

Dudley, P. (2007). The Lesson Study Model. Centre for Learning and Teaching, Newcastle University, December 2007. http://www.teachingexpertise.com/articles/the-lesson-study-model-of-classroom-enquiry-2950

Dudley, P. (2011a). Lessons for learning: how teachers learn in contexts of Lesson Study. PhD thesis, University of Cambridge.

Dudley, P. (2011b). Lesson Study development in England: from school networks to national policy. *International Journal for Lesson and Learning Studies*, 1(1): 85–100.

Dudley, P. (2013). Teacher learning in Lesson Study: What interaction-level discourse analysis revealed about how teachers utilised imagination, tacit knowledge of teaching and fresh evidence of pupils learning, to develop practice knowledge and so enhance their pupils' learning. *Teaching and Teacher Education*, 34: 107–21.

Edwards, A. (2005). Let's get beyond community and practice: the many meanings of learning by participating. *Curriculum Journal*, 16(1): 49–65, DOI: 10.1080/0958517042000336809

Fernandez, C. (2002). Learning from Japanese approaches to professional development: The case of lesson study. *Journal of Teacher Education*, 53(5): 393–405.

Fernandez, C. (2005). Lesson Study: a means for elementary teachers to develop the knowledge of mathematics needed for reform-minded teaching? *Mathematical Thinking and Learning*, 7(4): 265–89.

Fernandez, C., Cannon, J. and Chokshi, S. (2003). A US–Japan lesson study collaboration reveals critical lenses for examining practice. *Teaching and Teacher Education*, 19(2): 171–85.

Fernández, M.L. (2010). Investigating how and what prospective teachers learn through microteaching lesson study. *Teaching and Teacher Education*, 26: 351–62.

Fernández, M.L. and Robinson, M. (2006) Prospective teachers' perspectives on Microteaching Lesson Study. *Education*, 127(2): 203–15.

Gao, X.A. and Ko, P.Y. (2009). 'Learning Study' for Primary School English Teachers: A Case Story from Hong Kong. *Changing English: Studies in Culture and Education*, 16(4): 397–404.

Garet, M., Porter, A., Desimone, L., Birman, B. and Yoon, K.S. (2001). What makes teacher professional development effective? Results from a national sample of teachers. *American Educational Research Journal*, 38(4): 915–45.

Groth, R., Spickler, D., Bergner, J. and Bardzell, M. (2009). A qualitative approach to assessing technological pedagogical content knowledge. *Contemporary Issues in Technology and Teacher Education*, 9(4): 392–411.

Gu, L. and Wang, J. (2006). School-based Research and Professional Learning: An innovative model to promote teacher professional development in China. *Teaching Education*, 17(1): 59–73.

Gurl, T. (2011). A model for incorporating lesson study into the student teaching placement: what worked and what did not? *Educational Studies*, 37(5): 523–8.

Hart, L. (2009). A Study of Japanese Lesson Study With Third Grade Mathematics Teachers in a Small School District. *STRATE Journal*, 18(1): 32–43.

Holmqvist, M. (2011). Teachers' learning in a Learning Study. *Instructional Science*, 39: 497–511.

Holmqvist, M., Brante, G., Tullgren, C. (2012). Learning Study in pre-school: teachers' awareness of children's learning and what they actually learn. *International Journal for Lesson and Learning Studies*, 1(2): 153–67.

Huang, R. and Bao, J. (2006). Towards a model for teacher professional development in China: Introducing Keli. *Journal of Mathematics Teacher Education*, 9: 279–98.

Huang, R. and Li, Y. (2009). Pursuing excellence in mathematics classroom instruction through exemplary lesson development in China: a case study. *ZDM – The International Journal on Mathematics Education*, 41: 297–309.

Hunter, J. and Back, J. (2011) Facilitating sustainable professional development through Lesson Study. *Mathematics Teacher Education and Development*, 13(1): 94–114.

Inoue, N. (2011). Zen and the art of neriage: Facilitating consensus building in mathematics inquiry lessons through lesson study. *Journal of Mathematics Education*, 14: 5–23.

Isoda, M., Miyakawa, T., Stephens, M. and Ohara, Y. (2007). *Japanese Lesson Study in Mathematics: Its Impact, Diversity and Potential for Educational Improvement*. London: World Scientific.

Jansen, A. and Spitzer, S.M. (2009). Prospective middle school mathematics teachers' reflective thinking skills: descriptions of their students' thinking and interpretations of their teaching. *Journal of Mathematics Teacher Education*, 12: 133–51.

Kotelawala, U. (2012). Lesson Study in a method course: connecting teacher education to the field. *The Teacher Educator*, 47(1): 67–89.

Kriewaldt, J. (2012). Reorienting teaching standards: learning from lesson study. *Asia-Pacific Journal of Teacher Education*, 40(1): 31–41.

Lawrence, C.A. and Chong, W.H. (2010). Teacher collaborative learning through lesson study: identifying pathways for instructional success in a Singapore high school. *Asia Pacific Educational Review*, 11: 565–72.

Leavy, A.M. (2010). The challenge of preparing preservice teachers to teach informal inferential reason. *Statistics Education Research Journal*, 9(1): 46–67.

Lee, J.F.K. (2008). A Hong Kong case of Lesson Study – benefits and concerns. *Teaching and Teacher Education*, 24: 1115–24.

Lewis, C. (2009). What is the nature of knowledge development in lesson study? *Educational Action Research*, 17(1): 95–110.

Lewis, C., Perry, R. and Friedkin, S. (2009). Lesson Study as Action Research. In S.E. Noffke and B. Somekh (eds) *The SAGE Handbook of Educational Action Research*. London: Sage, pp. 142–54.

Lewis, C.C., Perry, R.R. and Hurd, J. (2009). Improving mathematics instruction through lesson study: A theoretical model and North American case. *Journal of Mathematics Teacher Education*, 12(4): 285–304.

Lewis, C., Perry, R. and Murata, A. (2006). How should research contribute to instructional improvement? The case of lesson study. *Educational Researcher*, 35(3): 3–14.

Lieberman, J. (2009). Reinventing teacher professional norms and identities: the role of lesson study and learning communities. *Professional Development in Education*, 35(1): 83–99.

Lim, C., Lee, C. Saito, E. and Haron, S.S. (2011). Taking stock of Lesson Study as a platform for teacher development in Singapore. *Asia-Pacific Journal of Teacher Education*, 39(4): 353–65.

Lo, M.L. and Pong, W.Y. (2006). Catering for Individual Differences: Building on Variation. In M.L. Lo, W.Y. Pong and C.P.M. Pakey (eds) *For Each and Everyone: Catering for Individual Differences through Learning Studies*. Hong Kong: Hong Kong University Press.

Marble, S.T. (2006). Learning to Teach through Lesson Study. *Action in Teacher Education*, 28(3): 86–96.

Marble, S. (2007). Inquiring into teaching: lesson study in elementary science method. *Journal of Science Teacher Education*, 18: 935–53.

Matoba, M., Yoshiaki, S., Reza, M. and Arani, S. (2007). School–university partnerships: a new recipe for creating professional knowledge in school. *Educational Research Policy Practice*, 6: 55–65.

Meng, C.C. and Sam, L.C. (2011). Encouraging the Innovative Use of Geometer's Sketchpad through Lesson Study. *Creative Education*, 2(3): 236–43.

Mercer, N. (1995). *The Guided Construction of Knowledge: Talk amongst Teachers and Learners*. Clevedon: Multilingual Matters.

Mercer, N. (2000). *Words and Minds: How We Use Language to Think Together*. London: Routledge.

Ministry of Education (1952). Zhongxue Zanxing Zhangcheng [Secondary school provisional regulation]. Beijing: Ministry of Education.

Norwich, B. and Ylonen, A. (2013). Design based research to develop the teaching of pupils with moderate learning difficulties (MLD): Evaluating lesson study in terms of pupil, teacher and school outcomes. *Teaching and Teacher Education*, 34: 162–73.

Ono, Y., Chikamori, K., Shongwe, Z.F. and Rogan, J.M. (2011). Reflections on a mutual journey of discovery and growth based on a Japanese–South African collaboration. *Professional Development in Education*, 37(3): 335–52.

Ono, Y. and Fereirra, J. (2010). A case study of continuing teacher professional development through lesson study in South Africa. *South African Journal of Education*, 30: 59–74.

Oshima, J., Horino, R., Oshima, R., Yamamoto, T., Inagaki, S., Takenaka, M., Yamaguchi, E., Murayama, I. and Nakayama, H. (2006). Changing teachers' epistemological perspectives: a case study of teacher–researcher collaborative lesson studies in Japan. *Teaching Education*, 17(1): 43–57.

Paine, L.W. and Fang, Y. (2006). Reform as a hybrid model of teaching and teacher development in China. *International Journal of Educational Research*, 45(4): 279–89.

Pang, M.F. (2006). The Use of Learning Study to Enhance Teacher Professional Learning in Hong Kong. *Teaching Education*, 17(1): 27–42.

Pang, M.F. and Marton, F. (2003). Beyond 'Lesson Study': comparing two ways of facilitating the grasp of some economic concepts. *Instructional Science*, 31: 175–94.

Parks, A.N. (2008). Messy learning: Preservice teachers' conversations about mathematics and students. *Teaching and Teacher Education*, 24(5): 1200–16.

Parks, A.N. (2009). Collaborating about what? An instructor's look at preservice Lesson Study. *Teacher Education Quarterly*, Fall: 81–97.

Pedder, D. (2006). Organizational conditions that foster successful classroom promotion of learning how to learn. *Research Papers in Education*, 21(2): 171–200.

Pedder, D., James, M. and MacBeath, J. (2005). How teachers value and practice professional learning. *Research Papers in Education*, 20(3): 209–43.

Pedder, D. and Opfer, V.D. (2013). Professional learning orientations: patterns of dissonance and alignment between teachers' values and practices. *Research Papers in Education*, 28(5): 539–70.

Pella, S. (2011). A situative perspective on developing writing pedagogy in a teacher professional learning community. *Teacher Education Quarterly*, Winter: 107–25.

Perry, R.R. and Lewis, C.C. (2009). What is successful adaptation of lesson study in the US? *Journal of Educational Change*, 10(4): 365–91.

Plummer, J.S. and Peterson, B.E. (2009). A preservice secondary teacher's moves to protect her view of herself as a mathematics expert. *School Science and Mathematics*, 109(5): 247–57.

Puchner, L.D. and Taylor, A.R. (2006). Lesson study, collaboration and teacher efficacy: Stories from two school-based math lesson study groups. *Teaching and Teacher Education*, 22(7): 922–34.

Puchner, L., Taylor, A., O'Donnell, B. and Fick, K. (2008). Teacher Learning and Mathematics Manipulatives: A Collective Case Study About Teacher Use of Manipulatives in Elementary and Middle School Mathematics Lessons. *School Science and Mathematics*, 108(7): 313–25.

Quicke, J. (2000). A New Professionalism for a Collaborative Culture of Organizational Learning in Contemporary Society. *Educational Management Administration & Leadership*, 28: 299–315.

Ricks, T.E. (2011). Process reflection during Japanese lesson study experiences by prospective secondary mathematics teachers. *Journal of Mathematics Education*, 14: 251–67.

Roback, P., Chance, B., Legler, J. and Moore, T. (2006). Applying Japanese Lesson Study Principles to an Upper-level Undergraduate Statistics Course. *Journal of Statistics Education*, 14(2). http://www.amstat.org/publications/jse/v14n2/roback.html (Accessed 23 February 2012).

Robinson, N. and Leikin, R. (2012). One teacher, two lessons: the lesson study process. *International Journal of Science and Mathematics Education*, 10: 139–61.

Rock, T.C. and Wilson, C. (2005). Improving teaching through lesson study. *Teacher Education Quarterly*, 32(1): 77–92.

Saito, E. (2012). Key issues of Lesson Study in Japan and the United States: a literature review. *Professional Development in Education*, 38(5): 777–89.

Saito, E., Harun, I., Kuboki, I. and Tachibana, H. (2006). Indonesian lesson study in practice: case study of Indonesian mathematics and science teacher education project. *Journal of In-service Education*, 32(2): 171–84.

Saito, E., Hawe, P., Hadiprawiroc, S. and Empedhe, S. (2008). Initiating education reform through lesson study at a university in Indonesia. *Educational Action Research*, 16(3): 391–406.

Saito, E., Khong, T.D.H. and Tsukui, A. (2012). Why is school reform sustained even after a project? A case study of Bac Giang province, Vietnam. *Journal of Educational Change*, 13: 259–87.

Salomon, G. and Perkins, D.N. (1998). Individual and social aspects of learning. *Review of Research in Education*, 23: 1–24.

Schwille, J., Dembele, M. and Schuburt, J. (2007). Global Perspectives on teacher learning: improving policy and practice. Paris: IIEP-UNESCO.

Sibbald, T. (2009). The relationship between lesson study and self-efficacy. *School Science and Mathematics*, 109(8): 450–60.

Sims, L. and Walsh, D. (2009). Lesson Study with preservice teachers: lessons from lessons. *Teaching and Teacher Education*, 25: 724–33.

Stigler, J.W. and Hiebert, J. (1999). *The Teaching Gap: Best Ideas from the World's Teachers for Improving Education in the Classroom*. New York: The Free Press.

Tsui, A.B.M. and Law, D.Y.K. (2007). Learning as boundary-crossing in school–university partnership. *Teaching and Teacher Education*, 23: 1289–301.

Tsui, A.B.M. and Wong, J.L.N. (2010). In search of a third space: Teacher development in Mainland China. In Chan, C.K.K. and Rao, N. (eds) *Revisiting the Chinese Learner, Changing Contexts, Changing Education. CERC Studies in Comparative Education*, 25(3): 281–311. DOI: 10.1007/978-90-481-3840-1_10

Villegas-Reimers, E. (2003). *Teacher Professional Development: an international review of the literature*. Paris: IIEP-UNESCO.

West-Olatunji, C., Behar-Horenstein, L. and Rant, J. (2008). Mediated Lesson Study, collaborative learning, and cultural competence among early childhood educators. *Journal of Research in Childhood Education*, 23(1): 96–108.

White, A.L. and Lim, C.S. (2008). Lesson Study in Asia Pacific classrooms: Local responses to a global movement. *ZDM International Journal of Mathematics Education*, 40: 915–25.

Yang, Y. (2009). How a Chinese teacher improved classroom teaching in Teaching Research Group: a case study on Pythagoras theorem teaching in Shanghai. *ZDM International Journal on Mathematics Education*, 41: 279–96.

Yarema, C.H. (2010). Mathematics teachers' views of accountability testing revealed through lesson study. *Mathematics Teacher Education and Development*, 12(1): 3–18.

Ylonen, A. and Norwich, B. (2012) Using Lesson Study to develop teaching approaches for secondary school pupils with moderate learning difficulties: teachers' concepts, attitudes and pedagogic strategies. *European Journal of Special Needs Education*, 27(3): 301–17. DOI: 10.1080/08856257.2012.678664

Yuk, K.P. (2011). Critical conditions for pre-service teachers' learning through inquiry: The Learning Study approach in Hong Kong. *International Journal for Lesson and Learning Studies*, 1(1): 49–64.

Chapter 3

Leading Lesson Study in schools and across school systems

Jim O'Shea, Sue Teague, Gill Jordan,
Jean Lang and Peter Dudley

In this chapter we report interviews with four pioneering leaders of Lesson Study (LS) in the UK. Jim O'Shea and Sue Teague are head-teachers who have overseen the development of LS in their own schools to a point where it is now embedded as the mainstay of professional learning and school improvement processes. Gill Jordan and Jean Lang are system leaders. Gill Jordan has considerable experience of working with groups of schools as they introduce LS and Jean Lang, a senior leader in a local authority, has overseen the development of LS across a large shire council. She has also introduced LS across the country in 'coasting schools' supported by leading teachers. Most recently she has developed LS in the London borough of Camden – which now leads the capital and probably England in the extent and depth of implementation and integration of LS into its school improvement processes.

Dudley (2011) conducted research into the experiences of primary school leaders using LS in their schools. This research explored:

a. how the headteachers legitimised LS amongst staff as a valid activity to pursue the selection of LS groups;
b. the degree to which LS groups exercised autonomy and the degree to which headteachers had sought to influence the focus and work of the group;
c. the extent to which LS had changed practice and improved pupil learning in the school;
d. how LS groups' activities contributed to improvement of teaching, learning and curriculum within schools;
e. the principal management and resource issues that the use of LS raised for school leaders.

Wider level

f. the extent to which these heads viewed LS as a distinctive form of professional learning for teachers;
g. the extent to which, in their views, LS provides value for money and justifies the degree of effort and disruption (for instance to release teachers) that it entails;
h. any policy implications they identified.

We will firstly offer some reflective insights from this research, and then we will let the interviews given by four of the authors of this chapter speak for themselves. Our words are thus offered for your direct interpretation.

Leading Lesson Study in schools

Before we begin it is worth reminding ourselves of the important findings of Professor Vivienne Robinson and her colleagues whose now infamous meta-study investigated the relationship between schools leaders' actions and pupil outcomes. Surprisingly (for some) she concluded that the single most impactful action that a school leader can take to improve educational outcomes for pupils is to take part in collaborative enquiries into improving teaching and learning (Robinson *et al.*, 2009). And the good thing about this is that LS is a straightforward form of collaborative enquiry for improving teaching and learning.

That said, for many school leaders and system leaders, introducing LS successfully is clearly a challenge. How so? For a number of reasons. Clearly LS takes some organising. The school timetable, staffing arrangements, the one teacher: one class model, funding arrangements – all of these make it awkward for three teachers to spend an hour in the same lesson three times. But they don't make it unaffordable or impossible. Let's face it, in a standard lesson study comprising three research lessons, the only contact time that actually needs staff cover is on the three occasions that two of the teachers leave their classes for up to an hour (usually less) while they observe the research lessons.

In our interviewees' views, this is a price well worth paying. They all argue that LS should be viewed not as an extra activity but as a core activity – the way we do professional learning – and that it should thus be costed into a school's budgets accordingly.

For some school leaders LS is not predictable enough. If you have identified an improvement and agreed with your governing body that it is a priority, it feels easier and more straightforward rather than embarking on reflective enquiry like LS, instead to send someone on a course and then tick the box – job done! LS, by its very nature, throws up surprises. That is one of the reasons that it is so powerful. They are often surprises to which the school is otherwise blind. So, as a head-teacher using LS, you need to be prepared for that – to be able to live with a certain level of uncertainty because that reflects reality. We encounter Jim O'Shea's views on this as he talks about the 'unintended outcomes' of LS in the first interview.

Dudley (2011) suggests that headteachers who have engaged in LS themselves are highly likely to succeed in leading it. They can use their prior LS experience of learning about pupils' learning and of applying that new knowledge to the design of iterative lessons, to the way that they legitimise LS, to the way they choose those teachers who will become early allies and advocates of LS and to the way they involve and win over the opinion formers, or the more experienced but perhaps initiative-overloaded members of staff who have perfected the art of keeping their heads down until the latest fad has passed. But heads who get it working well do not duck the issue of the quality time that people need to do it well and to get the most value from LS.

> The challenge is releasing teachers for the amount of time that they have to have for lesson study to work. It's the planning time and the unpicking of the lesson and the refining. That time is so important in the process that you can't just ask them to do that ... 'Oh, just meet together for 15 minutes after school' or 'Just have a chat about it in your lunchtime'. That dedicated time for them to. I think you have to ... as a head you have to make it em ... You have to let people know how valuable you think it is. Because you are putting a lot of resources and time – time and money – into it. So you have to be involved. You have to be interested. Otherwise it could be something that people have a lot of release time for but, you know, it's not going anywhere and it's not impacting on the rest of the school.
>
> (Dudley, 2011: 192)

The headteachers in this study prioritised time for quality conversations – for the 'unpicking' of the teaching and its effects on pupils' learning. Interestingly also, they did not feel that additional funding should be provided for LS activity. They regarded LS as core business – standard operating procedures of the school – which are provided for through professional development and performance management and their associated cost centres.

The leaders were also adamant that the three research lesson cycle is absolutely essential because of the cumulative growth in each lesson of knowledge creation and of the impact of this knowledge on pupil learning. The rewards from the second and even more so of the third research lesson are vastly greater and more impactful than those of the first research lesson (Dudley, 2011). So it is far better value for money to do the full three-lesson cycle, than to cut corners and just do one or two.

Schools are increasingly inter-leaving their performance management observations with lesson studies. Some are making it an entitlement for each teacher to participate in one lesson study each year. So one might experience formal performance management observations for two of the three terms each year, but in the other term one would participate in a lesson study. The LS findings are made public – shared with colleagues as is the tradition with LS, and so accountability is still very much there just as it is in performance management. Arguably, more so!

I recently heard Dame Alison Peacock, one of England's leading primary headteachers and system leaders, explain the way that her school[1] approaches performance management and Ofsted inspections. Unlike many schools that keep a log of teaching quality grades to share with their Ofsted inspectors in order to demonstrate that they regularly monitor teaching quality, she said:

> We were asked for our grades of teaching quality. I had to explain that at Wroxham we do not grade our teachers for their teaching quality. Instead, we gave the inspectors access to the notes of our lesson studies. That way they could see the quality of the conversations we regularly have about our children's learning.
>
> (Peacock, 2014)

Yet again in summer 2013, Wroxham was judged to be 'outstanding' on all counts.

Another reason why we believe that some school leaders find implementing LS a challenge is that they find it hard to explain or justify to governors and parents in terms of the disruption it appears to cause. But our Japanese colleagues can teach us something about this. Japanese schools make booklets at the end of each year in which they publish their research lessons and their outcomes for parents, governors, the local community and neighbouring schools. This not only celebrates and widens understanding of what has been learned and achieved, it creates and reinforces understanding amongst the school community of the underlying value of LS to everyone – and most of all to the pupils. We have also seen examples of the way that Japanese schools make displays of their research lesson plans as they emerge. These are displayed in succession in the corridor leading to the staffroom and encourage staff conversations about the research lesson design. We have even advised some school leaders in the UK who may be having trouble getting a particular group of staff to engage with LS to persuade some of their more confident LS groups to conduct their planning and post-research lesson discussions at one end of the staffroom during a break or a lunch hour. And we have been told that their enthusiasm becomes infectious, eventually leading even hardened sceptics to try their hand in a lesson study.

Some of what we have reported here rings true in the two interviews that follow but each of these headteachers offers much more depth and texture as they describe the way they have developed a LS culture in their school.

Jim O'Shea interview

PETE: *Why did you want to develop LS in your school and what was it about LS that made you think it was right for St Aloysius Juniors?*

JIM: Like all schools we wanted to develop teaching and learning and it was about four or five years ago and our maths subject leader was studying for her masters degree and as part of the materials that came with that I read a paper about research that had shown the impact of Lesson Study on improving the teaching of maths.

So! Delved a bit deeper, and was impressed by what I saw. This whole concept of a forensic examination of what you are doing! And then I started to read more about the way that it encouraged professional dialogue and self-reflection.

So rather than just teachers just talking about what was *not* working, LS seemed to provide the means for staff to stop, step back, review other approaches and try them out in the classroom. So, in essence, it was allowing the staff to take risks.

It was also mentioned in the McKinsey Reports[2] (which I know were on a global scale), looking at the effectiveness of different improvement models around the world and how schools and education systems are organised for improvement. What it showed was that the most successful education systems and the greatest improvements were where the responsibility for professional development lay with the actual practitioners, so I thought we could apply this approach at a school level. Teaching was good, very good across the school and we wanted to take it to the next level and LS seemed to be the process – a structure – that we could apply in terms of our CPD.

PETE: *As a headteacher, why do you think this has been a success with your teachers in St Aloysius?*

JIM: Training and the other one is definitely time. Teachers have big workloads, and you are going to give them something else on top – so the statistical chances of that being done to the degree that you would want it to be done are very slim. So we began with a lot of whole-staff sessions on what LS was, outlining what the process was. We went onto the Lesson Study UK website and there were also some DfE materials as well. We used those handbooks, slimmed them down a little bit, made them a little bit more relevant for our context. The key thing was giving teachers the time to plan and then actually carry out the research lessons, record the evidence and most importantly to evaluate the impact and then to share the findings – there are a lot of costs regarding time but the payback in the long term I think is more than worth it.

PETE: *What difference has it made to children's learning and to teachers' learning?*

JIM: For the teachers' learning I'm going to quote John Hattie.[3] It is very straightforward – he talks about 'visible learning' and he does this big, cognitive meta-analysis of all the different factors that impact on successful learning. And what he identifies as having the biggest effect on pupil learning is when the teachers become learners of their own teaching. So you have to look at what you can and can't control in a school; there are your externalities and then there are the people that you have in the building who are there every day with the pupils – the teachers and the teaching assistants – and it's about making them as effective as they can be. And when they are in charge of their own learning, they are taking responsibility for the way that they improve their teaching. I think the evidence shows that's where you get the biggest returns.

One of the things that has most improved *pupil learning* as a result of our lesson studies is active listening.

One of the things that I really like about LS is the unintended outcomes. You shine a light on something and the more you look the more you will find. There has been a lot of talk about pupil voice, but actually LS is a real vehicle to find out about the children's perceptions of themselves as learners. For us it was particularly around listening to what our children described as a good listener – the gap between what we thought they were doing and what they were actually doing and what they perceived 'listening' to be was cavernous, so our children literally thought that if you put your fingers on your lips and you are not saying anything, you are listening. When we talked to them to assess whether they had listened it was fairly apparent that they hadn't listened at all. So we did a whole school piece of work around active listening and that then impacted on practices across the school.

PETE: *I love the way you say that one of the things you love about LS is its unintended outcomes because that's what scares a lot of people about it.*

JIM: It does. But I think you have to embrace those unintended outcomes because we have this so-called monitoring and evaluation review system and self-evaluation but that all becomes very rigid and focused on outcomes that can be measured, whereas LS gives you a lot more qualitative information about what your children are actually doing in terms of learning in the class.

For *teacher learning* – I think the key thing is that CPD becomes JPD [joint practice development] i.e. not something done to you anymore, but something that's carried out in collaboration with a group of practitioners providing a clear structure and process, but which ultimately assigns them the responsibility for their professional development. And then there's the peer accountability that LS brings, sharing your findings and working through a process together, which is a very powerful element as well.

PETE: *What have been the biggest threats to making LS business as usual?*

JIM: Staff! We did have a couple of changes at critical times – the person who was leading on it left, then the lead teacher left and then the maths leader then went on maternity leave. So what I have tried to do is spread the load out in terms of who has the knowledge and the information, so that if we lose one part of the chain there will be other people who have got that knowledge and I can then hopefully spread them out to fill the gaps.

The other big challenges are time and money but for any head-teacher who raises this, what I would say is – it's about 'transition'. You can't just keep piling new things on. You have to be honest and say the model of professional development we were using at the time was of its time but now we are going to stop that and this is the way that we are now going to develop our staff professionally. And that then feeds into – informs the school's priorities in terms of finance and resources and how as a leader you plan in terms of time and commitments.

PETE: *If I was a headteacher about to start LS but I could not find the non-contact time to make it happen, what would your advice be?*

JIM: We did an audit of all the non-contact time we were paying for. There were a lot more people going out on external courses and we looked at the value of that in terms of sustainability. It's a bit like Dylan Wiliam's teacher learning communities. Teachers make thousands of decisions a day and they get into routines. What LS does is to give them a chance to step out of that, look at themselves and their practices and adapt what they are doing. To do that you need to give them time and space to almost take the third position on what you are doing. So you do have to make commitments regarding time: you have to look at who is flexible – because some-times you have to front-load the cover which can be a challenge as you may have two or three people out at once. So it's about how you use your more flexible members of staff for those key moments of time where you might only have one hour and you have three staff out of class, so again – it's planning ahead.

The lesson study is plumbed in.

We normally plan half a term to a term ahead and when we do our half-termly maps the lesson study is always the first thing that goes in. All this also goes on the school's shared annual calendar so that people can't plan other things where LS is scheduled. And I also control the supply budget so I determine where that goes.

PETE: *When you talk about 'flexible people' who do you mean?*

JIM: Me, the deputy headteacher and other cover.

PETE: *And do you find it's worth doing the cover yourself? Is it good use of your time?*

JIM: Yes. My Year 5 [ten year olds] teachers recently did some LS work using a new LS 'workbook'. The way it was structured meant that they could see a clear process from they changes they'd brought about, and the impact of that was that it highlighted something that we have been becoming aware of in our school which was the confidence of our more able female mathematicians. What that LS did was to confirm and reinforce this, which spurred us on to revisit that particular area because we have devoted the time to it and they have then followed it through and the findings are very clear.

PETE: *If you left, do you think LS would live on here?*

JIM: I hope so – the structures and resources are there, the tradition or routines are plumbed in. We have a half-term map and a yearly map; we have a cycle of development and LS is part of the way we do things.

I would hope that if I left, staff would say 'Are we doing LS this term?' So that once a year everyone has that chance to step back, do some research to reinvigorate the way they approach their teaching. Rather than just reacting all the time, I think LS gives you the chance to get ahead of the tide and see what everyone else has been doing so that you can then adapt the way that you do it to best meet the needs of your pupils. (I would probably come back as a governor as they can hold everyone to account!) (Laughs).

PETE: *Do your governors know about LS?*

JIM: LS has been explained to them, and in terms of the CPD report for the year they certainly know and understand the two most commonly used acronyms in our school: LS and TLCs (Lesson Study and Teacher Learning Communities). The key delivery models for professional development at St Aloysius Juniors are those two forms of joint practice development.

My hope for the Camden Lesson Study is that we will develop a web-based, single point of entry that we can go to and that will be our vehicle for identifying issues and we can then find a lesson study on it.

I would sum up by saying it's all about quality first teaching and pupil outcomes within the school context. It's about making teachers the best that they can be. As Michael Fullan says, teachers can be very individualistic and territorial. Knowledge is sticky[4] so what LS does is to make that knowledge widely available and more accessible.

There is almost too much research knowledge available at the click of a button nowadays – it can feel overwhelming. So if you are a teacher, LS gives help to understand that intractable issue that you have got with your class which you may talk about in the staffroom but never have the opportunity to do anything about. And it will help you to pick the most promising solution from all those available because you understand the issue better. So LS gives you the chance to step up and make a change.

I also acknowledge that there will sometimes be difficulties for heads who are introducing LS for the first time, and what I would say to them is that it's all about looking at what you don't need anymore and taking something out. And then getting LS in there, because in the long term it will pay dividends.

Sue Teague interview

PETE: *Tell me why you wanted to develop LS at Caddington and why you think it was right for Caddington?*

SUE: It was the words 'research base' that first appealed to me and the idea of working with a university. LS appealed to us as a school because it focuses on learning more than it does on teaching, and it focuses more on pupils than it does on teachers. We felt as a senior leadership team (SLT), that LS was about improvement and development rather than just about accountability, which there seems to be a lot of in education at the moment!

LS allowed us to build a community of practice and to strengthen our staff team. Our school has teachers in it who teach children from age three to thirteen, so we knew that we had to be inventive and to find ways of getting them to work together. Teachers will often stay in their own little boxes, whether that's departmental or in age phases. So it gave us a chance to provide people with direct experience of age phases they are not familiar with as teachers.

We also wanted to share and learn together as staff. We felt it was about developing from within. Not people going out on a course but actually learning from each other and finding out things about our own school, about our own pupils, and about our own learning establishment that we could then work on and improve. So it would, if you like, enable us to do some extremely focused reflection. It would also enable us to build a research-based environment – which is something that I thought would really help to improve the school.

PETE: *What was it that made LS a success with your teachers and school as a whole?*

SUE: We did the preliminary round of LS as a senior leadership team ourselves. We tested it out with the SLT and had some very honest discussions about how we thought it would work with the staff. For the first round of LS I think we did something quite brave – we firstly removed the SLT from the observations and secondly, we put everything else on a plate for the staff, so that the logistics were planned out in minute detail and they could concentrate on the LS itself. So everybody knew who they were going to be working with, where and when they were going to be working. The paperwork was tight too. We made it easy but at the same time we took the SLT out of the process. SLT members were on hand in an advisory capacity but only because we wanted staff to truly believe it was about them focusing on pupils and that it really was nothing to do with performance management or accountability; nothing to do with appraisal. With hindsight I think it was a good decision.

We also had clear protocols that staff developed with us so they knew them and were comfortable with what was going to take place in the classroom and how the post-lesson discussion would work. We were clear about our expectations in terms of outcomes and we asked everybody to present their lesson studies to the rest of the staff at the end of the LS round, and again we made it clear that we thought everybody should do that.

We also let staff choose the case pupils in the first round. We let them do that because we thought they would have a reason for following up anything they found out about and that it would stimulate their curiosity. We made sure that there was a rapid turnaround of their findings so all the paperwork was pulled in, discussed, then turned around so that the collective outcomes were put back in front of them when they were still fresh.

Importantly, we shared the reasons why we were doing it; we shared a bit of the history of LS, we talked about the school improvement plan, we talked about us shifting to become a research-based environment. Also, we wanted to make it enjoyable, so we didn't put strict notions on how the presentations should be and I can honestly say that when they did that first round of presentations I was proud! Really proud – of the quality of research that they produced. They were creative, they had worked as teams, they'd had fun and they had really looked at kids in more detail than had ever been done in this school before.

So, it was good fun and there was a real feel-good factor in the room on that presentation day, and that's important for teachers.

PETE: *How do you organise LS now it is part of the school's routine?*

SUE: We have been using LS for just over two years and this is the fourth round. The first round just involved the SLT and was part of the University of Exeter project. But since then the whole staff has done more lesson studies. They have just completed their third round and in every round everybody has taken part.

   We run two rounds a year.

PETE: *What have been the outcomes for pupils' learning and teachers' learning?*

SUE: When we started we really wondered what would come out of it and I think for pupil learning there have been two really important whole-school strategies that have come out of the first rounds of LS. This happened because it helped us to see things we had not been able to before.

   The fact that they have developed from *within* our school has been significant; from *within* rather than from an external initiative. They are going to sound really simple perhaps, but they are relevant and are applied in every classroom and because we have ownership of them they are having a real impact on pupils' learning.

   One of them is a strategy that we have called 'See, Hear, Clear' It sounds obvious, but every child in the room must be able to see; every child in the room must be able to hear what the teacher is saying or hear each other; and their learning environment needs to be clear from clutter or anything distracting. This is actually quite difficult to engineer and we have become much more aware of our learning environment: staff are more conscious of that than they ever have been. That's at every level – including me.

   When I talk to the staff in a staff meeting I now even run through 'See, Hear, Clear' in my own head. It's so easy to assume in the classroom that you as the teacher will have a favourite place to stand, you will maybe have a favourite place to sit and you will not even be aware of that. We discovered this was true through our lesson studies, and I think that as a result of LS we are all much more cognisant of that now. We make sure that the kids can do all of those things. There is a poster displayed in every classroom that says 'See, Hear, Clear'. We have also given pupils the responsibility to say if they can't see or hear, or if something is bothering them.

   The most recent round has led us to a focus on what, at the moment, we are calling 'Self'. We are still trying to nail it down precisely, but it's about pupils becoming self-motivated, self-aware, self-confident, self-sufficient and self-controlled. And we have tried to hinge the findings around these four or five key areas that we are just developing now.

Staff have been really excited about it and it was prompted by the massive amount of information that we had gathered from all the lesson studies. One of the assistant heads pulled together all of the findings about where we could improve which she then streamlined into four or five bullet points. The findings will be hinged around the word 'Self' and will be shared with staff and pupils.

I think that it's important to be able to distill the key findings of the research. So, we have developed two key initiatives which tackle things that we have discovered are hindering our pupils' learning. But we do have more work to do about how to involve pupils in closing the loop on what the lesson studies have thrown up.

PETE: *What has been the impact on teacher learning?*

In terms of teacher learning, teachers now believe that they are responsible for their own and for each others' CPD. So again, they are not looking externally; CPD is no longer seen as going on a course. This originally came out of a staff survey a couple of years ago, where staff thought that CPD was a weakness of the school because they thought it was all about going on courses. And it was hard to find courses that could move us as a school in one direction because of the range of people we have working here. So teachers are now more responsible for their CPD; they believe they can find the answers to questions. They also believe that they can find the answers to our own school improvement, and that they have both a responsibility and the ability to do that. And that has been really exciting! So we have a whole range of other research questions now emerging from the staff that are independent of LS and that people are asking for research time to pursue and also school visits in order to investigate them.

In terms of organisational learning, I would say there is a much greater awareness of learning in different phases which is brilliant. We have a unique learning environment here, ten years of education – four key stages from Foundation Stage to Key Stage 3, all in one place; people believe they can now understand that learning journey and they know they can walk around the school and talk to colleagues in other key stages about learning and they can go and observe it in their own time. They also can see for themselves that it is perfectly possible to switch phase as a teacher if that's what they want to do. We do a staff audit at the end of every year and some people have requested more teaching time in another key stage, some staff have even switched phase completely.

As a school leader, this is helping me to build a much more flexible learning environment, which in the times of change that school is currently experiencing is going to be quite important. People often have a fear of teaching age groups that they don't normally teach. But because of the way lesson studies have spanned year groups and key stages, that fear is now broken down and teachers see the fact that kids are just kids and that it is learning that is the important thing. Through LS we have removed the apprehension that teachers felt.

We are currently preoccupied with preparing for the new curriculum, and because of the focus on learning that LS has created, it has made us look more closely at progression because we have now developed an awareness of learning and of where the kids have been before and where they are going next.

PETE: *At Caddington LS has become 'business as usual' practice: so what have you done and what can other people learn from that?*

SUE: From the beginning, what we have wanted to come out of LS has been a change in the school's culture around CPD to make it more research informed. I think it was a very simple thing that we wanted to do, but in this country there is a gulf between teachers and academics, and I think we knew that existed and the academic world felt like a long way away from us. But we still felt there was value in trying and I think because we were clear we wanted to close that gap and work in a much more research-based way. So it was a simple ambition but a difficult thing to achieve. Adherence to that goal as the first thing, being very clear about it, giving time to it and having a very strong CPD leader in-house who believes in that goal as much as I do has helped – as did involving the SLT from the word go. If one person or a headteacher tried to introduce LS by themselves it would be very difficult.

Having a SLT who are all experienced in LS has been vital. All of my SLT did a lesson study and as a result they all believe in it. They have all felt that micro-level observation of the kids and they have all experienced the value of it at first hand.

One of our very good, but quite didactic teachers, described his first round of LS and the subsequent planning that happened as being like an iceberg because 90% of the work going into the lesson was 'underwater' – it had gone into the planning. And for the first time he found himself in a situation in lesson where he was not working as hard as the kids were. That was a great moment for him. Because the lesson had been so well set up by him and the other members of the LS group that rather than him doing all the graft at the front of the class, he discovered that he could go round listening to children, finding those gaps in their learning and plugging them there and then, on the spot. And to find that out for himself was great. He was a very experienced teacher and he was shocked at how much he had not seen happening in front of his eyes in his usual teaching – as are all of us are who have experienced LS.

PETE: *How have you made it affordable?*

SUE: The cost is important. We spent £2,300 on the last round of LS which sounds a lot, but when you consider that it reached all 30 members of staff in our school, then it isn't that expensive. When you consider what the school got out of it in terms of improved outcomes, I would say it was well worth it.

And now that we are more experienced in using LS we are very clear about how it works, and so we have got quite slick. We tell the kids that we have a round of LS coming up. We have tried approaching it in lots of different ways. In the last round we went for one big hit! So we did all our research lessons on three consecutive Mondays and we had supply teachers in throughout – 16 supply staff in on one day. But we did not have a single behavioural problem or any complaints from parents, because we had prepared everybody through two different key stage assemblies, that we were doing LS on those days. Pupils knew that it would be different – that they would not have their regular teachers and that other teachers would be observing in class. Even supply staff were buzzing because they were part of the morning briefing so they all knew that they were part of the team and were fascinated by it.

I think that making LS 'business as usual' at Caddington has hinged around having a few key people who believe in it because they have done it themselves. There must be an honest and open dialogue about how it would best work for your school. I do believe in staying true to the purity of LS though. It is *not* the same as peer observation or 'triad learning'. We developed a clarity about that as well and we knew therefore what outcomes we wanted for the school.

Having LS on three consecutive Mondays, when research lessons one, two and three took place, worked well for us. It provided time for people to have their post-lesson discussions in staff meeting time or scheduled meeting time and so we did fund time for that. But we either provided cover or scheduled staff meeting time for LS meetings. You cannot do it on the fly and expect people to use their lunch breaks or just have a couple of people meeting while others submit written notes. We stayed true to giving people the time. The paper work was pre-prepared for them. Planning and logistics are always very tight and prepared up to a year in advance. It's important to keep reminding staff about why they are doing it so they remember and value the process. I am clear why I am doing it but there are always new initiatives for teachers, so it is important to keep on reminding them.

There is still as much buzz here as when we introduced it and less apprehension. I still love it and am still discovering wonderful nuggets about learning. I went into the last round because somebody was off sick in the middle lesson. I went in and was able to pick up the observation of pupils because the notes from lesson 1 were so clear – and I found out the most amazing thing about the way a particular pupil was trying to learn to tell the time and the way she was computing. To watch it unfold in front of me after all these years in education and to be able to share what I'd observed with other staff was really interesting. The way her mind worked around learning 'time' was fascinating and the teacher would have missed it. The teacher asked her a question and the answer she gave to the teacher was so illogical that the teacher just said 'Okay' and walked away. It was only because I had seen the pupil's whiteboard with her calculations – so I had written it down and had taken a photo. When I explained her thinking afterwards in the post-lesson discussion, we were all amazed – you don't get better than that – to be able to go back into the classroom and discover something fundamental about a child's learning that no one in the school had been able to pick up before. We knew immediately how to improve her progress – but we wouldn't have without the LS.

PETE: *What advice would you give a school leader who is about to introduce LS?*

SUE: I think if you believe in your staff and you believe that they have got the ability to generate improvement but that they need a vehicle to do it, then LS will work for you. If you want to build a school community that focuses on children and on learning then LS is for you.

I would say it's not expensive. School improvement will cost you time and money but LS in particular gives your school a singular direction to go in, it makes teachers believe that they can, observing themselves and each other without threat of judgemental accountability. There are feelings of being accountable but they come from self-reflection rather than from monitoring. I would also say the thrill of finding out the features of good learning in your own pupils and sharing them in your own school is worth every penny and every minute spent.

Leadership of Lesson Study within and across groups of schools and school systems

The potential prize of establishing LS across a whole school system is enormous. Once the habits and routines of system-wide LS have become part of the rhythm of a community of schools, teachers start to demand their rights to learn through LS. If that learning extends to initial and newly qualified teachers, then this becomes self-perpetuating because LS becomes something that teachers expect to encounter and value as of right and from the earliest points in their careers.

Local systems of schools, teaching school alliances, school trusts, local authorities and universities are beginning to explore the rewards that can be gained when teachers not only share their practice across classrooms in a school, but also across schools in a system. In Chapter 6 of this book Hiroyuki Kuno illustrates the gains that can be made when these processes are established, and in her interview below Jean Lang highlights the importance of the role of 'knowledgeable others' – coaches, advisers or skilled academics who work with LS groups in order to enhance the facility of their LS processes and discussions in order to generate new knowledge and practice and to cross-fertilise what is happening from school to school.

But we in the UK are still a long way from this. Bringing people out of their own schools to participate in lesson studies with colleagues from other schools has been tried and has failed to take root a number of times (and I have been involved in several of these attempts). But each time we learn more about how to achieve the critical mass that will help LS take flight one day in a school system and flourish under its own steam as it does in Japan and as it is beginning to do in Singapore, Hong Kong, Indonesia, in pockets of Sweden, the US and the UK.

Gill Jordan has played this role of 'knowledgable other' amongst groups of schools in England. She has utilised LS in the development of writing and at the time of writing, she co-leads a large medical trial at Edge Hill University, investigating the use of LS as a vehicle for developing guided writing and mathematics.

Jean Lang has also played the role of knowledgable other and has grown LS-based networks across Lancashire. She has also led LS development across England through the National Strategies' Leading Teachers programme and more recently developed system-wide LS approaches in Camden.

In the following two interviews, firstly with Gill and then with Jean, we hear again many of themes that emerged in Jim and Sue's accounts such as the importance of having one or two headteachers who are personally experienced in LS. But we also hear about the need for system leadership, dissemination, the value that can be added within a system approach by 'knowledgable others' to coach and facilitate LS. And we also hear about the way that pre-existing collaborative arrangements can prepare the ground for cross-school LS and about the adoption of LS into local system-routines, local professional development and school improvement strategies and local publications, and even locally searchable online lesson studies.

Gill Jordan interview

PETE: *What for you has been the secret of orchestrating LS across a group of schools?*

GILL: In my view for this to succeed it is essential that there is somebody in the group of schools who has a very clear lead role and who is able to lead the group and to some degree manage it in its initial stages, and who is somebody who has a good understanding and knowledge of LS and professional learning in the wider field.

Where the schools were already working together in some way, either in geographical networks or working around a specific theme, I think that because they had already got relationships established it made it easier to start the LS work.

But for schools with no history of working together, I think there are real difficulties in working across each other from the outset. That led to a lot of difficulties in one project where, although there were enormous gains, that was more difficult because you had one teacher working from each of three schools together from the outset, without a deep understanding of what they were doing or even why they were doing it.

If I were to set that project up again, in retrospect I would advise them right from the beginning to take it more slowly. I think it would have been more useful to establish a LS group within each school first and then to do the work across schools. While some of those schools have continued to work together in LS, it isn't that many because it wasn't firmly established in their own schools first. So while the teachers themselves felt that they gained enormously from working in other schools, doing that alongside introducing LS is just a step too far.

I think it is critically important to involve headteachers or, in larger schools, a member of the senior leadership team who has responsibility for professional learning. If that doesn't happen, I think LS tends to be seen merely as a strategy that can be used in the short term – you do three research lessons which you might repeat a couple of times. But I don't see it as having any real depth in contributing to the ongoing professional learning.

But I have found that where headteachers have led LS successfully within their own schools they are in a good position to go on to work with a cluster of schools – especially if they know the cluster. I think this is a particularly valuable way of mobilising that knowledge.

In the current project that I am leading, when we have established that some schools are doing a really great job, we are linking them with schools that are having problems, so they can observe some of their research lessons in those schools. This is a variation on 'open house' research lessons.

Another thing that worries me is that sometimes teachers think that the research lessons are 'it'. They don't get the message that the research lessons are just the starting point; that it's the *learning* from those research lessons that should have a lasting impact on everything they subsequently do in terms of teaching. And I often think people don't get the fact that LS is much more than the three research lessons. LS has to be carried on from that to become a long term way of working.

PETE: *Has LS 'made a difference'?*

GILL: I don't think there is any doubt that it makes a difference in terms of both pupil progress and teacher learning. And I think in many cases schools report that there has been a real impact on learning even over a short period, and they have been surprised by that!

But I do think that there needs to be more work done in this area because I don't think enough schools think through at the beginning how they are going to assess and evaluate the success of interventions like LS in improving pupil progress and teacher learning, or in understanding its impact on pupils, or teachers – or in fact on the whole school. Although I do think this is beginning to improve.

The way that schools have often done this in the short term is to track case pupils. Schools that have been effective in doing that have tracked them in terms of looking at their levels in a particular subject area at the outset and then again at the end of the research lessons, and then at a couple of points further along the line to see whether the impact has been sustained.

PETE: *What has worked most successfully for you?*

GILL: Dissemination of the lesson studies amongst teachers is one thing, but also headteachers involving themselves in LS – both have been important.

Almost all schools disseminate their lesson studies within the school and feed back to their colleagues about what has happened and what has been gained through a lesson study, and that spreads enthusiasm and knowledge within the school.

If LS is led by an effective headteacher such as the headteacher at St Leonard's in Exeter who involved herself personally in LS, observed it, and thought carefully about where to start the next group off, then it is definitely possible through this approach to spread LS steadily throughout the school. Her school now has a very clear LS model and every teacher has the opportunity to become involved in LS, which has become embedded as the main focus of professional learning in the school.

But that doesn't always happen. So while dissemination within the school is extremely important in helping LS to spread, it needs to be led by an informed headteacher.

I think that giving groups the opportunity to observe LS in action, *before* embarking on it on their own, has also been a useful strategy. But again it needs to be informed by the knowledge of a leader who understands LS from the inside.

Videos demonstrating the process can be useful as well.

Using posters to capture and share the lesson studies with other teachers has been particularly useful in a group of schools. If you can do this, then in effect each teacher will gain insights from a larger number of research lessons all captured in the poster sessions, in which teachers capture what they have learned to share with other teachers. This approach is particularly useful for the teachers involved in the particular lesson study being shared, because it helps them to reflect upon what they have learned. But the posters are also useful for other teachers to observe and the posters can definitely give a 'taster' for those who aren't yet involved in LS.

I think capturing LS as 'case studies' is also a useful process for the people who write them because it clarifies their own learning. And people do read them, so I assume they are helpful to them as well – but I am not sure.

PETE: *What are your four top tips for making LS part of a school's standard operating procedures?*

GILL: Identify a school leader, or a leader across a chain or network of schools with deep knowledge and understanding of professional learning and of LS, who would manage an initial project across the schools. And then identify a lead person in each school with some experience or knowledge of LS, so that you have a team who already has a deep understanding of professional learning.

Provide high quality training for all the people involved in the way that I think we have done in terms of philosophy, process and protocols.

Ensure that before they start there are visits to schools with successful LS practice.

Have a clear plan for delivery of what you are going to be doing: identify an able and enthusiastic group of teachers; identify an area for improvement that is achievable and a priority for the school; identify at the beginning an effective form of evaluation of the impact on pupil progress and teacher learning; and then consider how you will scale-up from one group in each school in order to embed it more widely – and then work this up across the whole system.

Jean Lang interview

PETE: *What for you, has been the secret of orchestrating LS across a group of schools?*

JEAN: I think it is always very important for a group of schools to share some linked priorities, which then become the focus of the LS. Because then it's something *they* feel will have an impact on *their* own school. It's also good if those schools also have some kind of connection – that they have worked together collaboratively in some way before. It is possible to introduce LS when they haven't, but it certainly helps if they have had some kind of relationship before.

There also needs to be very clear leadership buy-in from head-teachers, and there needs to be somebody senior enough in the group of schools who knows about LS, who understands it and the benefits that it can bring to schools. It helps if one or more of the heads in the group of schools has actually participated in a lesson study, because that leader can convince the others that it's going to work. There will not be buy-in unless the leadership team in each school in the group feel LS is going to have a positive impact on teaching and learning and so that it isn't seen as just 'another thing to do'.

PETE: *And what about the work you did in the National Strategies with leading teachers and more recently with expert coaches in Camden?*

JEAN: If you have an expert working with a LS group in a school, or across a group of schools, then you need to be very careful about who that expert is because they need to be able to coach and to ask the right questions – they mustn't take control of the LS. I think that has clearly come out in our recent experience in Camden when teachers have become much more aware of what they have said in their LS discussions when they have videoed themselves as a group, planning and discussing their research lessons. They have been able to see how, for example, over-dominance by an expert can block another teacher in the LS group from coming to an understanding of why something has happened and how it could be improved.

So the mode of questioning by an 'expert' or 'knowledgeable other' – to probe or raise ideas and not to supply answers – is so important!

PETE: *What for you has been the impact of LS on pupil learning and standards and schools involved?*

JEAN: My first experience of working with LS was in Lancashire, working with a large group of schools in which 10 and 11 year olds were not making enough progress. LS made a huge, measurable impact on standards at age 11 in a very large local authority, particularly in writing. Nationally the improvement we saw was two times what it was in other schools.

The impact has been significant and lasting – not just in terms of learning but also on the quality of teaching. I noticed in a recent

Ofsted inspection report for one of the schools that had I worked with in Lancashire five years ago, that LS was still being used in 2013 and the inspectors commented on the positive impact it continues to have. I remember how that school became convinced that LS was the way to develop professional learning and quality of teaching and this is now clearly embedded in the school, even after a change of headteacher which shows it can become part of a school's routines.

In Camden we have several examples of schools where head-teachers are saying that they can see a really big improvement in the quality of teaching and it's because teachers are focusing far more on learning, they are far more aware of the learning of individuals and groups and they have much higher expectations of some children that they might not even have noticed before – the hidden children.

There is a project that we are doing in Camden at the moment, which is focusing on the Early Years – children aged two (or below) up to five years. I would say that this has probably been particularly successful because I think it has done something that has always been a challenge which is to bring together Early Years practitioners from schools and from children's centres and actually get them working together and talking about learning. There are often quite negative perceptions about what teaching is like in schools and what it is like in other settings which make collaboration and trust hard to achieve. But what we have had with LS is all practitioners working together, planning activities and focusing on talking together about what they have seen.

And they have all seen the same things across the board from babies to five year olds! For example, they have seen in all settings how adults do too much talking for too long and intervene too quickly in activities. And they have observed just how this actually limits learning because they are not allowing children to explore. They have also seen that practitioners are perhaps often afraid to let children take risks and so they prevent them from exploring resources sufficiently before they do a more structured activity with them. And this again limits the learning that a child can gain.

These observations have been consistent across both school-based settings and other settings. Discovering them collectively has already led to very significant changes in provision. We now see adults thinking about whether or not they should be intervening in an activity or about whether an activity they are planning really does give children choice and thus makes them have to think for themselves and discuss the choices in their own language.

Fewer, over-structured activities are being planned now and practitioners are consistently surprised at the developments that their children make when they are learning more independently.

This work is also having a massive impact in schools as well. If you look at the Early Years Foundation stage profile, elements such as confidence (a pre-requisite for later learning) are quite low in Camden. But through practitioners applying the knowledge that they are getting from these lesson studies, we are already seeing a big impact on children's confidence as learners and so it's likely to have an overall impact in Camden by increasing the number of children reaching a good level of development by age five.

PETE: *Can you tell us what are the most successful ways that you have found to get knowledge that has been discovered through lesson studies passed from one teacher to another in ways that they can use it in their own teaching?*

JEAN: The approach that we have taken in Camden has been to develop iterative, collaborative teacher learning across the schools – building on and connecting up the iterative, collaborative teacher learning that the teachers have been doing in their own schools through the lesson studies. We initially developed a model where teachers would conduct lesson studies in six schools involved in our original project and then meet with project leaders and subject consultants to share their outcomes and identify common points from which to learn more and to develop in the next phase. These were eventually turned into case studies and published on the web where they have been accessed thousands of times.

This initial work has now been transformed into a much bigger project that is about to become London-wide. What we have is people coming together each half term to work in action-learning sets to discuss their findings and feeding back to each other. The discipline of the action-learning set requires people to take turns to feed back what they learned in their lesson study while others actively listen, question, record and summarise. This structures the group conversations and facilitates cross-fertilisation of ideas as well as distillation of common themes and questions. It has been so successful that we have now utilised it in the Early Years project I was talking about earlier.

We are also moving into having 'master classes' in Camden, which are based on the Japanese 'open house' or 'public research lesson'. In our master classes, teachers keep a class back after school and then teach the particular approach that they have developed in their lesson study in front of an invited audience. They then discuss what they have been shown with the teachers and pupils involved. This is a new departure in Camden and a very exciting development.

PETE: *If you were advising a teaching school alliance that wanted to develop and use LS, what would be the key advice that you would give them?*

JEAN: I think this links with the first question in terms of making sure first of all that you have sufficient buy-in and by ensuring that those you work with understand what LS is and also have a clear understanding of the difference that it can make. You also need to deal at the start with any concerns about how it can be managed in a classroom by giving people ideas from experience. Others can back this up by giving examples of how they have done it, such as 'It was a surprisingly inexpensive way of making a real difference to professional learning in my school as well as to the quality of teaching and learning'.

Contrary to common misconception, I think LS is very cheap. And once leaders are convinced that it works, they find very imaginative ways of making it work, for example by using dedicated Planning, Preparation and Assessment (PPA) time. (There's a lot of planning, preparation and assessment in LS and there is no reason not to use it developmentally and collaboratively from time to time!)

From my experience, teachers are quickly convinced that it's going to work and they will take the time to do it because they know it's going to make a difference to their practice and ultimately to the children's learning. What is really interesting is that we only had a small amount of money in our current project budget for teacher supply cover. We thought people would want to cover classes in the early stages when teachers were observing research lessons, but we made sure that this was phased out before the end of the project so that LS was *not* dependent on the idea of additional funding by the end of the project. But in practice very few schools have asked for it, even in the first cycle of research lessons. I think this shows that if schools are committed to it, they build LS into their school improvement plans and their budgets. So rather than send someone off for training with no follow up, professional development is organised around LS cycles. They become the mechanism for mobilising new practice knowledge gained internally or from external inputs like courses.

So we don't abandon the idea of learning away from the classroom on courses, but we use fewer of them and when we do go on a course we use LS to make courses and in-house school improvement more effective. LS then makes a difference because you are going to apply what you have learned in a classroom and share what you have learned with others and that then improves practice not only in that school but also then across schools in the teaching school alliance or the local authority.

We are getting external recognition of this. Ofsted just recently inspected a school and said that the best teachers were the ones doing LS. This is the kind of thing that will convince even more people of the power of LS. But this kind of thing is not enough. It is also vital to evaluate the difference LS is making to children's and to teachers' learning.

For example, in Camden we have seen a very significant impact in standards in assessment and test results in mathematics as the numbers of children attaining Level 2b and at Levels 5 and 6 showed a marked increase. And these improvements were clearly linked to the mathematics lesson studies that we had been doing in the borough.

So in summary, I think it's about changing the culture across a group of schools and seeing schools as places where *research* takes place, so that you see professional learning in a different light. You see attitudes change from 'Let's go on a course' to 'We could go on a course but that could then give us ideas for improving learning that we could apply and develop using LS'.

Conclusions

We feel that the themes that these accounts have in common are striking. Successful leaders of LS within and across schools and school systems plan their approaches very carefully and give lesson studies a very high priority in the fabric and processes of the school or system – so that they are 'plumbed in'. These leaders communicate relentlessly before, during and after the lesson studies have taken place and they make sure that the outcomes of the lesson studies inform future planning and are shared with the school community. They understand the cost and the cost–benefits of the lesson studies and they amplify the impacts of the lesson studies by sequencing processes of alignment (of learners, needs and priorities) and by orchestrating what is learned, gained and shared through the lesson studies. Thus, they create even greater capacity for improving learning through LS (Dudley, 2014).

If you are a leader who is using this book with your leadership team, you could use these interviews for the purposes of carrying out a collaborative analysis of what can be learned from these accounts and responses, and how what you can learn from them could be tailored and applied to the context in which you are introducing or further developing LS.

Notes

1 Wroxham Primary School and Teaching School Alliance, Hertfordshire, England.
2 McKinsey & Company (2007). *How the world's best-performing school system come out on top*. London: McKinsey & Company; Mourshed, M., Chijioke, C. and Barber, M. (2010). *How the world's most improved school systems come out on top*. London: McKinsey & Company.
3 Hattie, J. (2009). *Visible Learning: a synthesis of over 800 meta-analyses relating to achievement*. Abingdon: Routledge.
4 Brown, J. and Duguid, P. (2002). Organising Knowledge. In S. Little, P. Quintas, and T. Ray (eds) *Managing Knowledge: an Essential Reader*. Thousand Oaks: Sage, p. 28.

References

Dudley, P. (2011). Lessons for learning: how teachers learn in contexts of Lesson Study. PhD thesis, University of Cambridge.
Dudley, P. (2014). *Lesson Study: a handbook*. Cambridge: LSUK. http://lessonstudy.co.uk/lesson-study-a-handbook/
Peacock, A. (2014) In dispatches. The Role of Lesson Observation in England's Schools. Seminar, Teach First and The Teacher Development Trust, London, 13 January.
Robinson, V., Hohepa, M. and Lloyd, C. (2009) School leadership and student outcomes: identifying what works and why. Auckland: New Zealand Ministry of Education.

Chapter 4

How Lesson Study helps teachers of pupils with specific needs or difficulties

Annamari Ylonen and Brahm Norwich

1 Introduction

This chapter discusses some of the key findings from a two-year development and research project in England, Raising Levels of Achievement for Pupils with Moderate Learning Difficulties (MLD), to be called Lesson Study-MLD project. One of the larger aims of the LS-MLD project was to improve the learning experiences and opportunities of pupils identified as having MLD to enhance their educational achievements and to develop pedagogic strategies, programmes and materials for wider use in secondary schools. This project, which ran from 2010 to 2012 and was funded by the Esmée Fairbairn Foundation, involved the training of over 60 teachers from about 30 secondary schools from the South-West and South-East of England in the Lesson Study (LS) methodology.

LS is a general strategy that exemplifies features of a professional learning community (Deppeler, 2012) as it can be used in different phases and areas of education (stage, curriculum area and student characteristics). However, it has tended to be used in certain subject areas, such as mathematics and science education, but not specifically with students identified as having special educational needs (SEN) or disabilities. Despite its general applicability, we have found no references to its previous use in developing inclusive teaching of students with SEN or disabilities in ordinary school and class settings. Although there is a tradition of inquiry-based approaches to inclusive developments (Ainscow, 2000; Howes *et al.*, 2009; Miles and Ainscow, 2011), these have not used LS practices and do not have the specific and intensive focus on class teaching and learning found in LS.

The project had several different aims and one of these – focused on in this chapter – was about developing the teaching and learning of pupils with identified MLD. The concept of MLD has not been well understood in theory or in practice and there has been a general lack of research about this group of pupils in schools in England (Desforges, 2006). The LS-MLD project aimed to change this by gathering research evidence about the characteristics of pupils who have been identified as having MLD and by raising awareness about MLD and the learning needs of these pupils. This was done by examining whether the LS methodology could help teachers in a number of mainstream and some special schools to develop their teaching approaches for this group of pupils and to raise the learning outcomes of these pupils.

The project was in two separate phases with different evaluation aims and rationales. In both phases the participating teachers first received training in the use of LS and were then asked to design and undertake a number of LS cycles in the broad areas of humanities, English and art (and some in the area of mathematics).

In phase 1 of the project the participating teachers undertook three LS cycles over two school terms and received ongoing help and guidance from project consultants. In the second project phase the teachers took two LS cycles over one school term and received less support from the consultants during their LS work in order to establish how the process would work in conditions more similar to those typical in schools. Although there were overlaps in the evaluation strategies, for example, relating to LS process evaluation which was carried out in both phases of the project, the emphasis in phase 1 of the project was on the concept of MLD and teaching strategies for MLD, while the emphasis in phase 2 was on analysing the learning outcomes of pupils after taking part in LS. It is not possible to discuss all the evaluation facets and research findings in this chapter – instead we will focus on a small number of themes which broadly relate to the barriers to learning of pupils who had been identified as having MLD and how LS could help to provide ways to improve the teaching and learning of these pupils.

The chapter is organised into three main sections. Section 2 briefly discusses existing research findings that are relevant to teaching and learning of pupils identified as having MLD – identification, teaching strategies and barriers to learning. Section 4.3 highlights some of the main findings of the LS-MLD project to illuminate how and why the LS process revealed aspects about teaching and about learning that helped to reduce the barriers to learning of the case pupils and other pupils in the classes. In the final Section 4 there is some discussion of the broader implications of the findings and general conclusions.

2 Barriers to learning

The Government's current definition of MLD which was used in this project, and which forms a part of the Special Educational Needs Code of Practice states that:

> Pupils with moderate learning difficulties will have attainments significantly below expected levels in most areas of the curriculum, despite appropriate interventions. Their needs will not be able to be met by normal differentiation and the flexibilities of the National Curriculum. They should only be recorded as MLD if additional educational provision is being made to help them to access the curriculum. Pupils with moderate learning difficulties have much greater difficulty than their peers in acquiring basic literacy and numeracy skills and in understanding concepts. They may also have associated speech and language delay, low self-esteem, low levels of concentration and under-developed social skills.
>
> (DfES, 2005: 6)

The definition makes reference to 'difficulties in understanding concepts' (what is sometimes also called low intellectual abilities) along with difficulties in literacy and numeracy and low attainments in most areas of the curriculum that cannot be addressed by teachers via normal differentiation practices. However, the boundaries between what is seen as constituting MLD and what is not are not specified and therefore judgements about what counts as MLD are hard to make using this definition (see e.g. Norwich and Kelly, 2005).

The concept of MLD remains poorly understood in theory and in practice. Evidence from the LS-MLD project, which further demonstrates the complex nature of the concept of MLD, has shown that about half of the pupils in phase 1 of the study of the total of about 60 pupils who had been 'officially' identified as having MLD did not meet the criteria for this category when assessed by a number of conventional measures such as the British Ability Scales (BASII). Many of these pupils had reasoning skills that were in the 'normal' range for the age group and only had lower literacy skills as compared to their peers (see Norwich *et al.*, 2013 for further details). Only those who had a statement of special educational needs came close to being in the lowest 2% of the age group in their reasoning and literacy skills – a conventional criterion used to assess children's intellectual functioning. This raises the question about 'within child' and 'within environment' barriers to learning where the former refers to barriers that are related to a child's cognitive functioning and the latter to barriers presented to a child's learning by the external environment.

Literature about MLD-related barriers to learning

Despite the category of MLD being one of the highest incidence categories of SEN in England, there remains a lack of research and developments relating to this area. As Norwich and Kelly (2005) point out, this could be related to the fact that there is no advocacy group for this group of children which promotes their needs and interests as well as raises awareness, as there are for groups of children who have various specific learning difficulties, such as dyslexia. However, there is some research evidence to suggest that pupils who have been identified as having MLD can follow broadly similar programmes as those without MLD and without a supplementary curriculum (Fletcher-Campbell, 2004). Although a small steps curriculum has been advocated by some for this group, others have seen this kind of differentiation as inadequate and propose more focus on problem solving, thinking skills and social interaction (Fletcher-Campbell, 2004). Generic strategies used for those with MLD might also be useful for others without MLD, a point which was relevant to the LS-MLD project in which most of the pupils with MLD were in ordinary mixed ability subject classes. This conclusion is in accordance with what Norwich and Lewis (2005) call the unique differences position as regards special pedagogy for pupils with SEN. According to this position, the MLD category has no specific pedagogic function, other than an intensifying of general teaching strategies relevant to other pupils.

Research about working memory – an ability to hold in mind and mentally manipulate information for short periods of time – suggests that pupils who have learning difficulties, including MLD, often also have poor working memory capacities (Gathercole and Alloway, 2007). Working memory is important in learning activities because it is related to the ability to remember and follow instructions. Because many learning activities require the use of working memory, pupils who have poor working memories are not likely to get the most learning benefit out of classes, which can lead to slowing down of their rate of learning. Gathercole and Alloway (2007) recommend an approach in which the teacher monitors and manages a pupil's working memory load in order to avoid overloading his or her working memory capacities and thus disrupting the learning process. Some of the strategies that teachers can use in the classroom to help pupils who have poor working memory capacities include the use of memory aids, rehearsal time, teachers repeating information, using simplified language and instructions and breaking tasks down into smaller chunks (Gathercole and Alloway, 2007).

3 Findings

In this section we will discuss some of the main findings of the LS-MLD project that are relevant to teaching and learning of pupils with MLD. The main questions that we address are:

- What did the LS process reveal about teaching and learning that could help to reduce the barriers to learning of pupils with identified MLD;
- How and why did the LS process do this?

The section is organised into three parts. The first part discusses the evaluation methods used in the research undertaken while the second part discusses the impact of the LS process on the teachers, for example, how the participating teachers developed new teaching strategies, developed constructive collaborations with colleagues, improved their planning of teaching, and gained better awareness of the pupils in the classes. Finally, the third part discusses the specific outcomes that participating in the LS-MLD project had on the pupils who had identified MLD.

Research methods

The evaluation methodology was informed by a Realist Evaluation methodological approach, based on the work of Pawson and Tilley (1997). Realist Evaluation aims to link three distinct broad aspects of a programme: its contexts, mechanisms and outcomes (C-M-Os) by constructing a programme theory that explains what processes (mechanisms) under what conditions (contexts) result in what outcomes. What characterises this evaluative approach is its realist model of causation that recognises context as critical to the operation of processes (mechanisms) that result in various outcomes (Pawson and Tilley, 1997).

Using previous LS and school improvement research literature and in consultation with LS specialists, a programme theory of LS was designed of C-M-Os at a school and a teacher level. The aim of a Realist Evaluation is to field test this theory to refine it in response to various data sources. In this evaluation the field test was done using a survey questionnaire and semi-structured interviews to triangulate the testing of the LS programme theory (Teddlie and Tashakkori, 2009).

In the final survey questionnaire 66 statements covering teacher and school-level contexts, processes and outcomes were formulated, which were rated using a four-point scale (definitely not; slightly; mostly; definitely; with a 'can't say' option). After piloting the questionnaire and revisions made, it was sent to 28 participating teachers at the end of phase 1 using an online survey tool (Survey-Monkey) and responses were received from 16 teachers from 11 different schools (57% response rate). At phase 2 of the project the survey was sent to 33 teachers and responses were received from 15 teachers from 10 different schools (45% response rate). In this paper attention is focused mainly on examining the outcomes of the C-M-O analysis and some of the mechanisms, but not the linkages that have been examined elsewhere (see Ylonen and Norwich, 2013 for more details about specific methods used).

The interview schedule covered teacher and school-level contexts, processes and outcomes with open-ended questions and probe questions to follow up responses. Nine semi-structured interviews were carried out in five schools in phase 1 and six interviews in three schools in phase 2 of the project. The teachers were chosen to represent the range of schools that had more and less challenging experiences of using LS, as identified by the LS consultants who supported the LS teams. Though there was neither time nor resources to interview all the teachers, the range of schools would illuminate the key LS processes. The interviews in schools were about one hour each and were all audio recorded, transcribed and thematically analysed (Robson, 2011). In this chapter, as with the survey data, only the outcomes of the C-M-O analysis are examined.

In addition, participating teachers completed LS case study reports, using a provided pro-forma, at the end of phases 1 and 2 to summarise what they had done and achieved during the process by focusing on one LS cycle as an example. In particular, the teachers provided the context and overall aims of the LS, a summary of each of the research lessons completed, the impact of the LS on pupil learning, on current and future teaching as well as on wider impact on the departments and school. Reports were received from 18 teachers from 13 schools that had completed phase 1 and from 19 teachers at 13 different schools that had completed phase 2. The reports were content analysed (Robson, 2011) for the goals of the LS undertaken and for details of the outcomes of the LS process for pupils, teachers and schools more widely.

The teachers also completed a questionnaire at the end of phase 1 of the LS programme, which was designed to elicit from teachers what specific teaching approaches and strategies they had used and developed through their lesson studies which focused on pupils with MLD as their case pupils. This questionnaire was completed by 22 teachers and the responses were thematically analysed.

Impact on teachers and teaching

This part discusses how the LS process enabled the teachers to develop new teaching strategies, more awareness of the case pupils' needs (and other pupils in the class) and to improve their planning of teaching and collaboration with colleagues. Our evidence shows that for most teachers on the project the LS process led to improved and more insightful teaching.

The teaching approaches questionnaire set out to examine what pedagogic/teaching strategies teachers developed for pupils who had been identified as having MLD through using LS in their classes. The questionnaire responses received from 22 phase 1 teachers showed that the teachers reported using many different strategies, which included specific approaches such as using visual aids, memory-enhancing techniques, motivation of the students as well as more 'traditional' approaches like using differentiated materials. The three most commonly used approaches were differentiation, multi-modal/sensory approaches and grouping and peer relationships/support (see Ylonen and Norwich, 2012 for more details). In general, differentiation was interpreted by teachers in a broader sense and not just as a way to provide different tasks for different students. Hence, such areas as providing a variety of resources for pupils with different learning styles, using different types of questioning and providing specific individual support were mentioned. Importantly, the teachers were not using a specialised MLD pedagogy, but instead were making use of generic teaching strategies that they adapted, extended and/or intensified in different ways for teaching pupils with MLD though the LS process. These strategies included and made use of various working memory approaches such as those recommended by Gathercole and Alloway (2007) discussed above in Section 2. The findings are consistent with a model of pedagogy that assumes that teaching approaches are extensions and intensifications of general pedagogic approaches (Fletcher-Campbell, 2004) and are consistent with the concept of a 'continuum of pedagogic strategies' as a position about the specialisation of teaching for pupils with SEN (Lewis and Norwich, 2004).

Table 4.1 shows the results of the LS process survey for both phase 1 and 2 teachers. It can be seen that the teachers were overall very positive about the outcomes of the LS process for themselves: in both phases the ratings were between 3.0 and 3.8 where 1 was the lowest and 4 the highest score. Most teachers agreed that taking part in the LS process had given them, for example, more confidence to make changes to their usual teaching approaches, a desire to try new and more novel approaches in teaching, the ability to be more open to learning from others and exposing their teaching to others as well as more ability to critically examine their own teaching. In addition, regarding pupils identified with MLD, the teachers felt that by taking part in the LS process their understanding of the learning needs of these pupils had increased, that they could better engage these pupils in lessons and that they could better plan and differentiate in their teaching for pupils with MLD (see Table 4.1).

The survey findings about the mechanisms of LS (see Ylonen and Norwich, 2013 for further details) also suggested that LS was seen to provide:

- collaborative opportunities to share knowledge and skills with colleagues;
- sharing of risk in innovating about teaching and more willingness to learn from errors;
- solidarity between teachers that affirms capabilities to innovate about lesson teaching;
- dedicated time to reflect, plan and problem solve in a supportive public setting;
- honest and constructive observations of research lessons to each other;
- a micro-focus on the learning of 1–2 students to enable a greater depth of analysis.

Table 4.1 Teacher-level outcome ratings, phases 1 and 2

Teacher outcomes	Phase 1			Phase 2		
	N	Mean	SD	N	Mean	SD
More confidence to try out novel teaching approaches in lessons	16	3.81	.40	15	3.60	.63
More willingness to make changes to usual teaching approaches	15	3.67	.62	15	3.60	.74
More theoretical and practical knowledge about LS	16	3.63	.62	15	3.80	.56
More able and willing to examine own teaching to become aware of false assumptions and new possibilities	14	3.57	.65	15	3.67	.62
More open to learning from others and exposing your teaching to others in safe settings	15	3.47	.91	15	3.60	.74
The LS process has improved the quality of planning of your teaching	16	3.44	.63	15	3.40	.74
Increased capability to engage pupils with MLD in their learning	16	3.44	.96	15	3.33	.72
Increased capability to plan and differentiate in your teaching pupils with MLD	16	3.44	.73	15	3.13	.74
More positive towards a dynamic concept of teaching as involving constant learning about how to deal with novel situations	15	3.40	.99	15	3.60	.74
Increased ability to articulate aspects of practice	15	3.33	.72	15	3.27	.88
More knowledge about how to overcome barriers to learning for pupils with MLD	16	3.31	.79	15	3.00	.76
More personal interest in providing quality teaching to all in your lesson planning and lessons	15	3.27	1.0	15	3.60	.63
More understanding about the nature and complexity of the learning needs of pupils with MLD	16	3.25	.86	15	3.13	.83
A more positive attitude to pupils identified as having MLD and to their inclusion in school and teaching	15	3.20	1.1	15	3.40	.74
Deeper knowledge about your curriculum subject and subject pedagogy for pupils identified as having MLD	15	3.07	1.1	15	3.07	.80

These survey findings are consistent with the analysis of the selected teacher interviews, briefly discussed below, which provided an insight into how the teachers came to see teaching in a different light during the LS process. A key aspect of this was getting to know the individual pupils identified as having MLD and what may have prevented these students from getting the most out of lessons. The interviews also highlighted that the teachers valued the observation process and teamwork aspect in LS as well as the ability to trial new teaching strategies and resources. There was much agreement among the interviewed teachers that the LS process created opportunities for them to develop their teaching practice.

Phase 1 teacher interviews

Two teachers from special school 1 pointed out that the observation process and the use of the video camera had been immensely helpful in making adjustments to existing practices. One of these teachers believed that she came to know the students' preferences better and so could better engage them, because she now had 'more empathy, more vigilance and more understanding' towards their needs. For the other teacher LS enabled him to tailor lessons to better suit the individual students, for example by the way of asking more questions. This teacher used LS to establish a more informal manner at the start of lessons that helped students calm down and settle into the lesson. These teachers attributed their increased confidence in risk-taking in teaching to LS. It is notable that LS was even seen to have these positive effects in special school lessons with small numbers of pupils, where there is more scope for flexibility and intensified lesson planning.

Teachers at secondary school 2 reported that LS had encouraged them to talk less while allowing the students to talk more. One teacher pointed out that the pupils identified as having MLD prefer an environment where they can be active in speaking and listening, which would increase their engagement in lessons. Both teachers agreed that observation and collaboration in the LS team had resulted in improved understanding of the learning needs of pupils with MLD, the sharing of ideas and the development of new teaching approaches.

Two teachers at secondary school 3 suggested that the observation process provided an insight into how different pupils react to different teaching strategies. Both teachers talked about the positive impact of the more meticulous planning of lessons on all students, not just those with MLD. In terms of new ideas about responding to MLDs, one teacher highlighted that the challenge to engage MLD pupils and other pupils in class – for example by using more exciting resources and using practical tasks – was found to be effective and that these methods would continue to be used in the future. The other teacher interviewed at the school brought up the importance of teamwork in the LS process by suggesting that:

> *The observing teacher is as important as the one delivering the lesson.*

She also took the view that the participating teachers in the LS team worked in a 'no blame environment' and had good working relationships, which meant that teachers could be honest in their observations and discussions. This teacher suggested that:

> *As planning has been meticulous for LS, it shows what impact this can have on lessons … extra planning pays off as the lessons are better as a result, even for an experienced teacher.*

She went on to point out that:

> *Looking at the specific needs of students means that you are more aware of the needs of all students.*

The first teacher remarked that the LS process had given an insight into teaching pupils with MLD in that:

> *It was interesting to see how students respond to different things. Initial assumptions were often wrong.*

At the fourth school, the two teachers suggested that watching and observing the students closely allowed them to develop strategies that were more tailored towards the needs of the pupils. The strategies implemented were often small, but had significant impact on the pupils with MLD, for example, by introducing a differentiated task in an art class, which helped the pupils with MLD to develop their drawing skills.

The teacher at school 5 also referred to the insights gained from observing the pupils in class and subsequently getting to know the pupils and how they think. The teacher reported that as a result of the LS process and the changes implemented in teaching practices, not only had the pupils with MLD benefitted with increases in their confidence and self-esteem, but the whole class had benefitted as a group. The teacher also emphasised the personal satisfaction derived from the practical relevance of the LS process which focuses away from government approaches, but gives more focus to wider learning:

> *Teachers often start with assessment criteria and work backwards and this does not allow things to be found out about wider learning.*

Another great benefit reported was that the process allowed teachers to take more risks than in normal lessons, which resulted in more innovative strategies being explored and increased teachers' understandings about the learning needs of MLD pupils who were often 'invisible' in classes.

Phase 2 teacher interviews

For a SEN specialist teacher in secondary school 1, the LS process had revealed new strategies with surprising effects on the pupils, many with extensive special educational needs. LS had also challenged preconceptions about what the pupils can achieve. This teacher particularly valued the observation process because it enabled new aspects to be discovered about the pupils' learning. She also pointed out that:

> *I'd seen them all as very needy in their own right and needing my support, but I think there's a point at which you can step back and allow them to support each other, and I hadn't really thought about that before.*

Two teachers from secondary school 2 had some contrasting views about LS. Although one saw some benefits in the LS process, particularly the collaborative aspects and becoming more aware of the specific needs of the pupils with MLD, she felt over-burdened by the amount of work involved. That the LS process was on top of her already heavy workload, overshadowed the whole LS experience for her. The other teacher, though recognising the extra work in the LS process, was more positive and suggested many beneficial outcomes arising from the LS process. This included more analysis of her teaching, LS team collaboration and introducing some new strategies 'that we can use to boost all students that have learning difficulties...'. She went on to suggest that as a result of the LS process, she had become more aware of how to observe the pupils in the class to see:

> *How they are developing and what they are finding hard and what's working or what's not working.*

For the two teachers and the deputy head at the third school the LS process had been a very positive and beneficial experience. Their views reflected many of those already reported above. For one of the teachers interviewed at this school, the LS process had:

> ...*just got us talking about MLD – I don't think we really talked about it before – we'd talked about those students who had serious learning difficulties, and we'd talk about the really bright ones ... whereas the MLD students we just didn't ... it has made us aware of them so actually we've started to think about them and how to put strategies in place to help them.*

The deputy head of the same school highlighted how the LS process had made the LS team think more about teaching strategies:

> *I think what it made us do was re-visit what was there and actually apply it ... what it highlighted was that you don't perhaps pay enough attention to the kids with MLD in your room – you kind of give them a piece of work and expect them to do their best with it rather than tailoring it a little bit more specifically.*

Case report data

An analysis of the teachers' case reports from both phases of the project, discussed below, shows that they saw the impact of the LS process on themselves as positive, for example, in terms of the planning of teaching and increased confidence to take risks. The evidence from the case reports supports the interview data discussed previously and demonstrates that taking part in the LS process created many positive teacher outcomes that are relevant to teaching and learning of pupils who have SEN.

The most common impact mentioned in 8 of the 17 phase 1 case reports (47%) was that LS enabled the teachers to trial and develop new teaching strategies and resources. The two next most common outcomes both mentioned in six case reports were, first, a general shift in focus of attention from the teacher and teaching to pupils and their learning, and second, teachers' increased awareness of the individual needs of pupils, including those with SEN. For example, one teacher commented that as a result of the LS process she had adopted a student-focused approach which meant that students had 'ownership of their own learning and time to reflect on what they have done'. Other types of outcomes (mentioned by three teachers) were, first, teachers' increased awareness of MLD and SEN more broadly, and second, impact on lesson planning and pedagogic styles. As an example of the former type of outcome, one teacher suggested that:

> *Lesson Study has been useful to identify two masking strategies used by students with MLD to disguise their difficulties; copying and rushing to finish.*

The words of the following three teachers are examples of the impact on lesson planning and pedagogic styles:

> *The process has encouraged us to take risks with our teaching in the future and to try ideas which take us outside our comfort zones.*
>
> *The main impact for me has been to think much more widely in my lesson planning to increase the variety of different activities with more making and doing tasks.*
>
> *The collaborative nature of the planning and evaluation has been great. The lessons developed as a result have been very effective in terms of pupils' learning. Even when they didn't go to plan, we have learned a lot from them.*

Analysis of phase 2 case reports, as in phase 1 reports, showed that the most common outcome for the teachers themselves was that LS enabled them to explore new teaching strategies and resources. This was reported in 15 of the 19 case reports (79%). For example, one teacher commented that:

> *Being able to plan with other subjects brought a range of ideas and strategies into my teaching which I would not have previously included.*

Also frequently reported was an increase in teachers' awareness of the needs of individual pupils with MLD and the importance of this new awareness (in eight reports). Teachers at one school who were hoping to continue using LS after the project ended, raised a view linking LS with dynamic assessment of pupil needs by suggesting that:

> *We see lesson study as an infinitely flexible method of tracking student progress and engagement – we will recommend it as a general*

diagnostic tool as well as a specific way of addressing the needs of SEN pupils. We think that a long-term use of Lesson Study would result in significant long-term improvements in achievement.

Phase 2 teachers also saw the benefits of the observation process (in six reports) and of collaborating in the LS team (in 5 case reports). For example, one teacher suggested that:

The LS process ... has highlighted some very important aspects that would not have come to light if I did not have other adults in the room observing what the class was doing.

Pupil outcomes

In order to determine what effect, if any, the LS process had on the case pupils who had been identified as having MLD two different approaches were used. The case reports filled in by participating teachers at the end of the process were used to analyse the main qualitative learning outcomes in phase 1. In phase 2 of the project more emphasis was placed on assessing pupil learning outcomes quantitatively using a method of Goal Monitoring and Evaluation (GME), which is briefly explained below (see Norwich and Ylonen, 2013, for more details about methods and findings).

The GME method has been used to evaluate the outcomes of many kinds of programmes in various service contexts, initially under the name Goal Attainment Scaling (GAS) (Jones *et al.*, 2006). Previous evaluation (Dunsmuir *et al.*, 2009) indicates that it is most dependable when it meets these criteria:

i   there is advance specification of the expected goal;
ii   at least three goals are used;
iii there is independent review/assessment of levels attained.

In the version of GME used in this project, the LS teams were asked to set two to three goals per case pupil before the LS cycle commenced. In addition, the teams were asked to specify three pupil performance levels on an 11-point progression line for each of the case pupils' goals (ordinal scale). These levels were defined in terms of the two to three goals: two before the programme started (a baseline level and an expected level), and one after the programme (an achieved level). In this way, the teachers assessed pupils' achieved levels by comparison with baseline and expected levels. They also gave descriptions for all three levels and evidence for those descriptions. The LS teams were also expected to set levels so that there was some moderation of the attained levels to avoid bias that may arise from only one teacher's assessment. The attained levels at the end of the LS cycle were then used to evaluate pupil outcomes in terms of any progress relative to baseline and the expected level (progress as expected; more than expected, less than expected or no progress). The degree of goal attainment could also be analysed in terms of the kinds of goals set.

The phase 1 case reports from 18 teachers outlined the main impact of the LS process on the case pupils with MLD as assessed by the teachers. The most common type of outcome reported in the reports was the beneficial impact of the LS process on the pupils' general behaviour and/or motivation, which was mentioned 12 times in the 18 reports (67%). Examples of the impact on behaviour were: 'pupils who had been reluctant to ask or answer questions grew in confidence throughout the LS process' and 'marked increase in confidence of the two MLD case pupils ... their attitudes to learning and participation have increased'. The reported outcomes focused largely on behaviour/motivation (over 70% of the outcomes mentioned) rather than on academic/cognitive skills, and were mostly in general terms rather than in specific terms.

At the end of phase 2 of the project, completed GME data were received from 9 of the 15 schools (several LS teams gave incomplete data while a few gave none). This comprised data from 14 separate lesson studies with one to two case pupils per lesson study. In total, teachers set 69 pupil goals in these lesson studies, which included the following, for example:

- to ask for help more frequently when struggling to understand;
- to be more engaged in class discussions;
- to develop written ideas independently;
- to be more confident in expressing viewpoints;
- demonstrate understanding of auditory and visual information.

Table 4.2 shows that out of the 69 LS goals, progress was met or exceeded in just over half of the goals (54%; 37 goals) as assessed by the LS teams. Out of these 37 goals, progress was as expected in 25% of goals (17) and more than expected in 29% (20) of goals. In just

Table 4.2 Goal Monitoring and Evaluation: 15 schools, 14 lesson studies, 69 goals set

Progress	Percentages
Progress as expected	25% (n = 17)
Progress more than expected	29% (n = 20)
Progress but not met the expected level	46% (n = 32)
No progress	0% (n = 0)
TOTAL	100%

under half of the goals pupils' made some progress that did not meet the expected level (46% or 32 goals). This shows that of all goals the case pupils made *some* progress from the baseline level.

Personal goals for pupils with MLD were analysed in terms of whether they were curriculum-subject related for example 'developing written ideas independently' or referred to a learning process for example 'being less disruptive and argumentative'. Some goals were both subject related and about learning process, e.g. 'independently offering contributions to class discussions and begin to record ideas in a more independent way' or 'being more frequently engaged in activities when emphasis is on using key vocabulary'. Overall, 49 of the 69 goals (71%) were about learning process only, while the remaining 20 goals (29%) were goals that were subject related or subject related linked to learning process (see Table 4.3). Table 4.3 also shows the level of attainment (scored 0–3 as shown in the table) by these three different kinds of goals. This indicates that the mean goal attainment scores for learning process and subject-related goals were alike and similar to the overall attainment scores (in the range 1.79–1.83). The mean score for the relatively few combined subject-related and learning-process goals was slightly higher at 2.0.

Table 4.3 Level of goal attainment by type of goal

	None (score = 0)	< Expected (score = 1)	As expected (score = 2)	> Expected (score = 3)	Total	Mean
Subject related	0	6	5	3	14	1.79
Learning process + Subject related	0	2	2	2	6	2.00
Learning process	0	24	10	15	49	1.82
TOTAL	0	32/46%	17/25%	20/29%	69	1.83

4 Conclusions and discussion

This chapter has discussed findings of a two-year development and research project in England with a focus on developing the teaching and learning of pupils with identified MLD in mainstream and some special schools. The aim of this concluding section is to highlight some of the key findings discussed in the preceding sections as well as to allude to further research that could be undertaken in this area.

This chapter has focused on two main questions that the research has been used to address: finding out how the LS process helped to reduce barriers to learning of pupils with identified MLD in the project schools (Question 1) and elucidating the reasons about how and why the LS process was able to assist in reducing such barriers to learning (Question 2).

As discussed above in Section 3, the LS process survey, the selected teacher interviews and the case reports showed that the teachers commonly felt that taking part in the LS process had given them confidence to try new approaches in teaching, that the collaborative aspects of the process had been beneficial and that their planning of teaching had improved. In addition, the teachers felt that by taking part in the LS process their understanding of the learning needs of pupils who had been identified as having MLD in their classes had increased and that they could better engage these pupils in lessons. The teachers also expressed a newly acquired awareness of the learning needs of all pupils in the classes, and not just the case pupils who had been identified as having MLD. The interview data brought to focus the benefits gained by the teachers engaging in the LS observation process and working across subject departments, which led to new insights about the case pupils' and other pupils' learning needs and preferences as well as teaching practices.

The pedagogic questionnaire findings showed that the teachers reported using many different strategies for teaching pupils identified as having MLD that were, by nature, generic and can be seen as strategies that teachers would have in their general teaching repertoire. Most importantly, the analysis about the pedagogic approaches used by teachers in phase 1 of the project indicated that there were no distinct or specific pedagogic approaches for pupils identified as having MLD that were not also relevant to others without MLD (e.g. low attainment or other SEN).

In phase 1 of the project pupil learning outcomes were only assessed qualitatively in the case reports written by the teachers at the end of the

LS process. The teachers reported many beneficial learning outcomes, which were largely behavioural-motivational such as improved pupil confidence, attitudes and engagement rather than academic-cognitive. The goal setting and monitoring introduced in phase 2 of the project made it possible for goal attainment to be examined for the individual case pupils following the LS cycle. Analysis of the GME data showed that there was progress from the start to the end of the LS cycle for just under half of the pupils with MLD at expected or beyond the expected levels. The rest made progress but less than expected. However, there was no assessment of these gains independent of the LS teams. Nor could the gains be strictly attributed to the LS procedures in general terms. Other evidence such as case reports, questionnaire and interview data suggested, however, that LS made some difference and this can be a basis for tentative causal inferences at a local level (Maxwell, 2004).

To summarise, the findings discussed in this chapter indicate that the LS process enabled teachers to develop teaching approaches via collaborative team planning and observation of teaching and learning, and to focus on the learning requirements of the pupils with identified MLD, who then showed some gains in their learning. Although the findings about pupil outcomes cannot be simply generalised to other settings, they act as a clear demonstration of positive pupil learning outcomes in a particular context and use of LS.

The findings of the LS-MLD project discussed in this chapter and elsewhere (see Norwich and Ylonen, 2013; Norwich *et al.*, 2014; Ylonen and Norwich, 2012, 2013) also raise many questions for further research. Such research could focus on the development of teaching of other groups of pupils with SEN, not just those with MLD, as part of the movement to develop more inclusive forms of teaching. Another line for further research could be directed at the general use of LS in schools, for example, in relation to the use of LS in pre-service teacher training (which is the subject of the following chapter in this book). There is also the prospect of undertaking experimental evaluations (Randomised Controlled Trials) to examine the effects of LS on the professional learning of teachers in a particular area of teaching. At the time of writing, we are involved in a small-scale trial at primary and secondary schools that examines how LS can be used for assessment purposes by developing a novel classroom-based 'response to teaching' method of assessing the learning needs of pupils who have difficulties in their learning. There are many opportunities to develop further research in LS, as, despite its widespread use in the Far East and increasing use in the USA and the UK, LS is generally at an earlier stage in its adoption in Europe as outlined in Chapters 1 and 2. The LS-MLD project was a step in that direction.

References

Ainscow, M. (2000). The next step for special education – supporting the development of inclusive practices. *British Journal of Special Education*, 27(2): 76–80.

Deppeler, J.M. (2012). Developing inclusive practices: Innovation through collaboration. In C. Boyle and K. Topping (eds), *What Works in Inclusion?* Maidenhead: Open University Press, pp. 125–38.

Department for Education and Skills, DfES (2005). *Data Collection by Type of Special Educational Needs*. London: DfES.

Desforges, C. (2006). *Review of literature about pupils with moderate learning difficulties*. London: Esmée Fairbairn Foundation.

Dunsmuir, S., Brown, E., Iyadurai, S. and Monsen, J. (2009). Evidence-based practice and evaluation: from insight to impact. *Educational Psychology in Practice*, 25(1): 54–70.

Fletcher-Campbell, F. (2004). Moderate Learning Difficulties. In A. Lewis and B. Norwich (eds), *Special Teaching for Special Children? Pedagogies for Inclusion*. Maidenhead: Open University Press, pp. 180–91.

Gathercole, S.E. and Alloway, T.P. (2007). *Understanding Working Memory – A Classroom Guide*. London: Harcourt Assessment.

Howes, A J., Davies, S.M.B. and Fox, S. (2009). *Improving the Context for Inclusion: Personalising Teacher Development through Collaborative Action Research*. London: Routledge.

Jones, M.C., Walley, R.M., Leech, A., Paterson, M., Common, S. and Metcalf, C. (2006). Using goal attainment scaling to evaluate a needs-led exercise programme for people with severe and profound intellectual disabilities. *Journal of Intellectual Disabilities*, 10(4): 317–35.

Lewis, A. and Norwich, B. (eds) (2004). *Special Teaching for Special Children? Pedagogies for Inclusion*. Maidenhead: Open University Press.

Maxwell, J.A. (2004). Causal explanations, qualitative research and scientific enquiry in education. *Educational Researcher*, 33(2): 3–11.

Miles, S. and Ainscow, M. (2011). *Responding to Diversity in Schools: An Inquiry-Based Approach*. London: Routledge.

Norwich, B. and Kelly, N. (2005). *Moderate Learning Difficulties and the Future of Inclusion*. London: RoutledgeFalmer.

Norwich, B. and Lewis, A. (2005). How specialized is teaching pupils with disabilities and difficulties? In A. Lewis and B. Norwich (eds) *Special Teaching for Special Children? Pedagogies for Inclusion*. Maidenhead: Open University Press, pp. 1–14.

Norwich, B. and Ylonen, A. (2013). Design-based research to develop the teaching of pupils with moderate learning difficulties (MLD): evaluating Lesson Study in terms of pupil, teacher and school outcomes. *Teaching and Teacher Education*, 34: 162–73.

Norwich, B., Ylonen, A. and Gwernan-Jones, R. (2014). Moderate Learning Difficulties – Searching for Clarity and Understanding. *Research Papers in Education*, 29(1): 1–19.

Pawson, R. and Tilley, N. (1997). *Realistic Evaluation*. London: Sage.

Robson, C. (2011). *Real World Research* (3rd edition). London: J. Wiley and Sons.

Teddlie, C.B. and Tashakkori, A. (2009). *Foundations of Mixed Methods Research: Integrating Quantitative and Qualitative Approaches in the Social and Behavioral Sciences*. London: Sage.

Ylonen, A. and Norwich, B. (2012). Using Lesson Study to develop teaching approaches for secondary school pupils with Moderate Learning Difficulties: teachers' concepts, attitudes and pedagogic strategies. *European Journal of Special Needs Education*, 27(3): 301–17.

Ylonen, A. and Norwich, B. (2013). Professional learning of teachers through a Lesson Study process in England: contexts, mechanisms and outcomes. *International Journal of Lesson and Learning Studies*, 2(2): 137–54.

Chapter 5

Lesson Study in initial teacher education

Wasyl Cajkler and Phil Wood

Since the early 1990s, initial teacher education (ITE) in England has been largely school-based and characterised by school–university partnerships. Over the course of a one-year postgraduate programme, student-teachers typically spend 24 of 36 weeks in schools, the remainder based in the partner university. At the end of the training year, national surveys regularly report high levels of satisfaction that increase each year (Teaching Agency, 2012). Nevertheless, as in other countries, ITE is challenged because 'what is taught in education classes is disconnected from teachers' work in the classroom' (Kotelawala, 2012: 67). Consequently, there is constant demand for change with successive Secretaries of State taking steps to shift responsibility for ITE to schools.

The most significant implication of school-based ITE is the importance of student-teachers' work with an experienced 'other' in schools, a supervisor or mentor responsible for the development of the student-teacher. The quality of this relationship and the opportunities it brings for a deep study of pedagogy are crucial to student-teachers' success. The mentor typically acts as guide, supporter, adviser, broker of learning experiences, encourager and motivator. A mentor also monitors subject knowledge and teaching skills development while sharing expertise about planning and teaching. Within such a complex task there is bound to be variability in teacher-student experience. Hobson *et al.* (2009), in their comprehensive review of the literature, reported high levels of satisfaction among student-teachers, the vast majority enjoying good support from mentors. However, the experiences of student-teachers can vary quite markedly from school to school and some studies have reported weaknesses in mentoring practice that have a negative impact (Hobson *et al.*, 2009: 210). Hobson *et al.* suggest that this may lead to a lack of adequate challenge from mentors with low-risk activities being assigned to student-teachers, trial and error learning and over-focus on craft skills with insufficient time for deeper study of pedagogy. Furthermore, what constitutes effective teacher education is a question of uncertainty (Hardman, 2009), which places near impossible demands on teacher educators (Ben-Peretz, 2001). Many approaches have been suggested: apprenticeship, applied science models, reflective practice, internships and school-based training with minimal theoretical input. In addition, there has been a raft of alternatives for example recent initiatives aimed at recruiting high-flyers, such as Teach First in England and Teach for America. Against this frequently changing background, we describe an innovative use of Lesson Study (LS) in ITE, an approach which helps both student-teachers and mentors to bridge the gap between what is taught in ITE programmes and what is practised in schools.

Lesson Study in ITE

With the continued uncertainty over the most advantageous approach to ITE, Farrell (2006: 218) argues that teacher education programmes should focus more on what it means to be a teacher and less on individual 'technicist' approaches, so that new teachers develop the ability to engage in 'anticipatory reflection'. It is argued that this reflective development enables student-teachers to respond to the diversity of their classes in pedagogically creative and confident ways. Hiebert *et al.* (2003: 202) similarly claim that prospective teachers need to be prepared for continual learning, not just 'equipped' with a set of teaching skills:

> The model we propose claims that it is both more realistic and more powerful to help prospective teachers *learn how to learn* [emphasis added] to teach mathematics effectively when they begin teaching. In other words, preparation programs can be more effective by focusing on helping students acquire the tools they will need to learn to teach rather than the finished competencies of effective teaching.

With such perspectives in mind, we have developed and piloted the use of LS with student-teachers of geography and modern languages, as part of a publicly funded research project. In partnership with several secondary schools, which volunteered to engage to use LS in teaching practice placements, we sought answers to the following questions:

- How does LS led by school-based mentors contribute to teacher development?
- What conditions favour the use of LS in a school–university partnership?

The principal aim was to field-test a model of LS, so it is not our purpose here to give a full detailed account of the research but to explain the model and justify its use in teaching practice placements. However, we refer to findings from the research to illustrate how the model operates and its effects on participants.

How has Lesson Study been used in ITE?

In order to situate our model, it is important to briefly review what existing research, reported in English, tells us about LS in ITE. A number of approaches (see Table 5.1) have been attempted outside Japan, for example in the US, Singapore and Canada, the majority on the teaching of mathematics. A smaller number have looked at science teaching and some have had a different focus, for example Rock (2003) on elementary school social studies, Sims and Walsh (2009) on early childhood education, Tsui and Law (2007) on teaching Chinese in Hong Kong. Chassels and Melville (2009) and Leavy (2010) worked with primary teachers in Canada and Ireland respectively.

Table 5.1 summarises the principal studies that include a cycle of LS involving classroom teaching during a student-teacher's placement. The studies exhibit variability and diversity in their application of LS with no single, agreed approach. 'Formal' LS closely mirrors the Japanese approach, namely the cycle of collaborative activity of planning-teaching-observing learning, evaluating and re-teaching. Some studies (for example, Chassels and Melville, 2009; Tsui and Law, 2007) appeared to achieve this, fully adhering to this formal model, but it is not always clear in the studies whether all student-teachers were able to participate fully. However, it is fair to say that studies in Table 5.1 succeeded in implementing LS cycles which resemble the original Japanese model. All of the studies include the essential features of collaborative planning, opportunities for teaching in schools with observations focusing on learners and their learning and some

Table 5.1 Examples of projects using a full cycle of LS including classroom teaching

Studies	Aspect of LS	Phase/subject	Examples of key findings
McMahon and Hines, 2008 (US)	LS cycle in 1 day	8 pre-service mathematics student-teachers; two 9th grade geometry classes	Collaborative reflection
Myers, 2012 (US)	Group LS cycle in practicum	20 elementary student-teachers; mathematics	Collaborative engagement but difficulty of promoting meaningful reflection
Ricks, 2011 (US)	LS cycle: peer teaching, followed by school-based teaching	Second year secondary mathematics course: four women	Deeper level of engagement; logistical challenges to implementation
Parks, 2008 (US)	Group LS: 1 lesson in school	27 interns; 12-week elementary school maths	Teachers' learning situated in classrooms is messy
Parks, 2009 (US)	LS cycle: 1 research lesson in school	3 interns; elementary teachers; writing	Participants collaborated but did not achieve significant learning
Marble, 2006, 2007 (US)	LS cycle of 3 lessons; groups of 3	24 elementary student-teachers, science teaching	Reflective approach to teaching, student-teachers relieved from performative pressures; purposeful collaborative practice, improvements in lesson design and delivery
Chassels and Melville, 2009 (Canada)	LS cycle in 4-week practicum	60 B.Ed elementary student-teachers; 20 associate teachers; 1 pre-service instructor	Deeper understanding of curriculum and pedagogy
Tsui and Law, 2007 (Hong Kong)	2 LS cycles over 4 weeks	2 student-teachers of Chinese; 2 mentors, 2 university tutors	'participants came to a new understanding of their roles in the activity system' (p. 1300) of a school placement
Leavy, 2010 (Ireland)	LS cycle, teaching inferential reasoning	26 primary school teachers, Ireland	Improvement in subject knowledge and approach to teaching
Rock, 2003 (US)	1 cycle: collaborative LS and individual approach compared	Elementary school social studies: 8 student-teachers	LS gives opportunities for thoughtful inquiry and learning how to teach
Davies and Dunnill, 2008 (England)	Learning Study: full cycle (university–school process)	33 student-teachers in Year 1; 36 in Year 2	Learning Study is practicable and beneficial in ITE; deepened understanding of teaching

collaborative evaluation of the research lesson. With variable success in terms of student-teacher development, they integrated LS into the practical experience of student-teachers.

A number of other approaches, in some measure different to the 'formal' approach, have been used but they stop short of teaching research lessons in placement classrooms. Fernandez (2005, 2010) evaluated Microteaching Lesson Study (MLS) in which prospective mathematics teachers plan and teach research lessons to their peers in teacher preparation programmes. This is credited with leading student-teachers to develop less teacher-centred pedagogy, moving from 'telling' approaches (2005: 42) to engaging students in 'discovery and construction of mathematics and concepts'. Other studies have also used collabora-tively planned peer MLS in order to explore the complexity of teaching (Carrier, 2011). However, it is not clear how lessons learned in MLS and such adaptations of LS translate to actual classroom practice. Table 5.2 (overleaf) summarises studies that have used adaptations of LS.

Such studies demonstrate that adaptations with a foundation in LS can be used to good effect to suit different contexts. Even where there were limitations in the application of LS, benefits were recorded. For example, Sims and Walsh (2009: 731), whose student-teachers taught research lessons but could not be observed by their mentors, concluded that engagement in an adapted form of LS can be effective in develop-ing reflective practice and reducing concerns about failing the teaching placement. Crucially, all the adaptations share an approach founded on collaborative consideration of learning, detailed planning for learning followed by collaborative evaluation.

What is also noteworthy from the literature is the relative absence of LS from ITE in the UK, the exception being Davies and Dunnill's use of LS in a one-year postgraduate programme. LS has emerged as an approach that uses LS underpinned by variation theory:

> The critical difference between learning study and lesson study lies in the presence of a learning theory which underpins the ways in which the teachers plan, implement and review the research lessons. The learning study approach is essentially a kind of lesson study with an explicit learning theory—the variation theory of learning.
>
> (Pang and Ling, 2012: 591)

This dearth of studies is surprising given the work of Dudley (DCSF, 2008) who introduced LS to primary schools as part of the Primary

Table 5.2 Examples of modified forms of LS in initial teacher education

Studies	Aspect of LS used	Phase/subject	Example of key finding reported
Carrier, 2011 (US)	MLS: pairs team-teaching to peers	57 student-teachers in Elementary science methods course; 4 case study participants	LS develops effective strategies for planning and teaching, analytical abilities, self-reflection, and fosters teachers as lifelong learners
Cavey and Berenson, 2005 (US)	Lesson plan study (LPS)	High school mathematics 1 woman	Enhancement of lesson planning ability; growth in mathematical understanding
Cohan and Honigsfeld, 2007 (US)	LS adaptation; peer presentations	17 early childhood science undergraduate and 51 graduate student-teachers	Useful tool for lesson planning and evaluation
Fernandez, 2010 (US)	MLS (planning and peer teaching)	18 prospective secondary mathematics teachers	Less teacher-centred pedagogy as a result of microteaching to peers
Gurl, 2010, 2011 (US)	Planning with mentor, followed by peer teaching	8 student-teachers of high school mathematics, 2 mentors	Discussions with mentors and peers of important ideas in mathematics
Sims and Walsh, 2009 (US)	University-based classroom teaching but no observation: video substitute for observation	32 pre-service early childhood teachers in Year 1; 25 in Year 2	LS affords 'a true glimpse of what it means to learn from teaching' (2009: 732)

National Strategies and Galanouli's (2010) recommendations to policy-makers for its use in Northern Ireland.

Conditions that favour the successful deployment of LS in ITE have also been identified, notably the engagement of mentors who have familiarity with the LS process and its aims (Gurl, 2011; Marble, 2006) and willingness by all participants to investigate practice and to question one's own assumptions about teaching and learning. However, there are challenges to integrating LS in ITE, for example:

- non-involvement of mentors or limited participation (there are several studies reporting this);
- mentors' lack of familiarity with LS (Marble, 2006: 92);
- teachers not being able to commit to 'formal LS' (Gurl, 2011) due to workload pressures;
- danger of shallow levels of reflection leading to inappropriate learning (Myers, 2012; Parks, 2009);
- over-mentoring resulting in unhelpful pressures on student-teachers (Tsui and Law, 2007).

Consequently, the obverse of the above favour the successful application of LS i.e. effective preparation of participants so they are familiar with the process, time for mentor engagement, collaborative deep reflection about planning, teaching and observation, and perhaps most importantly the courage to focus on students' learning in classrooms rather than the performance of the individual student-teacher.

In summary, there has been great variability in the methods and contexts in which 'LS'-style approaches have been used. Nevertheless, core activities and approaches emerge, and the general impression from the literature is that the use of LS with student-teachers can contribute positively to the effectiveness of teacher preparation.

Lesson Study: University of Leicester model

In the light of the above experience, we developed a LS model for field-testing with student-teachers of geography and modern languages (ML). Ten student-teachers and mentors volunteered for the project during first and second teaching placements, November–December and March–May respectively in the one-year programme. Each placement lasts eight weeks.

What is specific to the model and contrasts with many of the studies mentioned above is the central contribution of school-based mentors who lead the project and teach the first research lesson following collaborative planning with the student-teacher. In some schools, the student-teacher and the mentor are joined by another collaborating teacher; in others, the mentor and student-teacher work as a pair. The structure of this model, which draws on Dudley (2011) for many of the stages, is represented in Figure 5.1.

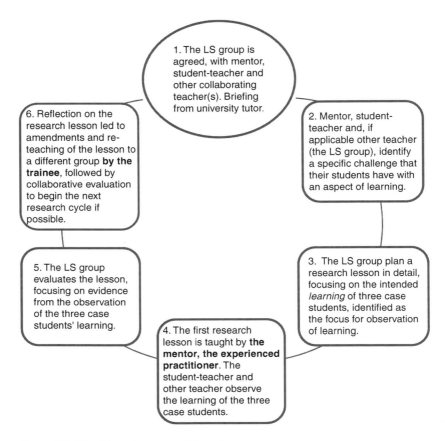

1. The LS group is agreed, with mentor, student-teacher and other collaborating teacher(s). Briefing from university tutor.

6. Reflection on the research lesson led to amendments and re-teaching of the lesson to a different group **by the trainee**, followed by collaborative evaluation to begin the next research cycle if possible.

2. Mentor, student-teacher and, if applicable other teacher (the LS group), identify a specific challenge that their students have with an aspect of learning.

5. The LS group evaluates the lesson, focusing on evidence from the observation of the three case students' learning.

3. The LS group plan a research lesson in detail, focusing on the intended *learning* of three case students, identified as the focus for observation of learning.

4. The first research lesson is taught by **the mentor, the experienced practitioner**. The student-teacher and other teacher observe the learning of the three case students.

Figure 5.1 Teaching placement LS cycle

The key task for university tutors in stage 1 is to familiarise mentors and student-teachers with the cycle of lesson planning, with particular attention given to learner-focused observation in research lessons. Induction into the process is done at specially convened training meetings and with the issuing of written guidance, including reference to the Lesson Study UK website (http://lessonstudy.co.uk/) and the *Lesson Study Handbook* (Dudley, 2011). Once the student-teacher starts the placement, however, the university tutor takes a back seat, responding to requests for advice but only attending the research lesson taught by the student-teacher (stage 6). When observing this lesson, the university tutor, like the mentor and any other observing teacher, focuses on the learning of two or three case students, identified collaboratively by the student-teacher and mentor. Significantly, the focus of observation is not directly on the performance of the student-teacher.

The length of the cycle depends on individual school circumstances but the minimum is a cycle of two lessons (the first taught by the mentor, the second by the student-teacher). In addition, the stages are subject to minor adjustment or refinement. For instance, in some schools, student-teachers interview or seek written feedback from the case students (an addition to stage 4 above). This stage is advised by Dudley (2011: 11) but optional in our model. Information gleaned from this feedback is used to inform the evaluation and the discussion of implications for future lessons.

Our evaluation of the model and its impact on student-teacher and mentor development was qualitative and inductive, drawing on analysis of recordings of mentors and student-teachers planning and evaluating research lessons, observation notes, DVDs of research lessons and lesson-plans/resources. At the end of the teaching practice, individual interviews with mentors and student-teachers were conducted to explore perspectives about professional learning in LS. Participants were asked to recall their engagement in LS and its consequences for the development of both student-teacher and mentors.

We used Communities of Practice as the lens to study the impact of LS. Communities of Practice share ways of interacting and thinking (Wenger, 1998), with mutual engagement an important guiding concept, representing a mode of belonging in social learning systems. Wenger (2000: 227) describes this as 'doing things together, talking, producing artefacts'. *Mutual engagement* in a collaborative LS project should, if successful, contribute to a sense of belonging in a community of practice. Our model enables student-teachers and mentors to work together in a *'joint enterprise'* (Wenger, 1998: 73) that binds them together with the purpose of developing 'a set of shared resources' or a *'shared repertoire'* (Wenger, 1998: 73). The concept provides a useful framework to evaluate the contribution of LS to the integration of student-teachers into the pedagogic practices of their departments. In a school placement, a student-teacher begins as a novice peripheral member of the department with his or her mentor as the central expert participant. However, the agency of the individual must not be lost in a Community of Practice perspective, because those involved all experience personal as well as collective learning from the process.

Evaluation of the model

Claims made in this chapter are informed by the experiences of five student-teachers of geography and five modern linguists and their mentors. Through engagement with these case studies, a number of insights have started to emerge. The model that we implemented enjoyed four important advantages over approaches reported in many previous studies:

1   following a university methods course that included collaborative planning and peer teaching, participants were able to attend detailed training sessions to learn about LS;
2   collaborative in-school planning of at least two research lessons targeting learners' needs (as in formal Japanese LS);
3   an LS cycle managed by the mentor who taught the first research lesson;
4   observation of learners known to the mentor but also to the student-teacher from the teaching placement, with time for discussion integrated into the teaching placement.

Perhaps the most significant of the above is the centrality of the mentor, but the four conditions suggest that it is possible to establish a strong and close variant of Japanese LS in school placements although there were challenges to its integration. The principal negative feedback from mentors was that the process is time-consuming. While acknowledging time constraints, all nevertheless argued that the project was worthwhile and should be continued. One mentor argued that it should become integrated into the general practice typical of school placements such as weekly meetings and reviews of materials, and that ways should be explored to make this possible. Organising dedicated time for planning and evaluation of the research lessons was essential. In most cases, ways were found to use existing ITE time (tutorials, weekly review time, lesson feedback time) for the preparation and evaluation of research lessons. Despite the constraints, most groups in the schools organised two preparatory meetings for each lesson. The typical pattern of a cycle was two research lessons but one school achieved two such cycles of two lessons and one did a cycle of three research lessons (the first and third taught by the mentor). Chassels and Melville (2009) included two research lessons in a four-week practicum and Tsui and Law (2007) managed two cycles of two lessons in four weeks, although the first cycle was pressured and very stress-inducing.

Interviews with participants suggest that LS allows for participative discussion about learning and teaching and opportunities for a collaborative approach to learning in a supportive community in which both mentors and student-teachers are learners focused on the improvement of pedagogy and not just on the training of the prospective teacher. Three themes emerged from mentor and student-teacher interviews, following comparative content analysis (Powney and Watts, 1987: 165–7) by two researchers:

1   the value of mentor and student-teacher collaboration in the co-planning and teaching of research lessons;
2   the positive impact of observation of learning in the classroom as opposed to focusing on individual teacher performance;
3   amendments to teaching attributed to the LS process which accompanied gains such as greater confidence, learner awareness and pedagogic understanding.

Planning meetings were facilitated by mentors who often used key questions to elicit ideas from the student-teachers. Content tended to be dominated by two issues which were the learning challenge, generally couched in terms of what learners find difficult, and approaches to teaching such as macro-structures of lessons and resources or tasks to be used. While student-teachers made fewer inputs to the conversation than mentors, they asked questions about lessons and about their structure, made suggestions that were accepted and did not report feeling intimidated:

> *I felt comfortable and confident ... I felt that my opinions would be valid ...* (modern languages student-teacher)

When reviewing lessons, both student-teachers and mentors can acquire new insights into what is happening in the classroom, as evidenced by the following exchange between a modern languages co-tutor and her student-teacher who was frustrated because she thought (wrongly) that student talk was off-task and potentially disruptive:

MENTOR: *All the kids I heard talking when you were talking, they were talking about the lesson and then they were generally trying to figure out what to do and what was going on.*
STUDENT-TEACHER: *I thought they were just like talking.*

MENTOR: *No. No. And that's what I've learnt from it, because I would have been exactly the same as you. I would have been at the front getting really frustrated thinking they were all talking and going off, when actually they weren't off-task. They were trying to figure out what the task was.*

Here, we see how the opportunity to observe pupil behaviour closely led to a change in the mentor's thinking and in the advice she could give to her student-teacher. The mentor described LS as revelatory:

It's just literally been a revelation for me. I've never really had the chance to sit with one of my groups that I teach and be able to get to know them in that way, because it's a shame really that there's not more room for it because I've learnt now that X ... has got quite a high sense of what's fair and what's not and that needs to be addressed...

Having qualified in the 2008–9 year, she complained during the interview that she had not experienced LS during her ITE year. Such was its impact on her.

In addition, mentors believed that student-teachers matured more quickly through LS than through an entirely traditional approach to the placement. The observation of a research lesson taught by a geography student-teacher (E) was assisted by the school's policy of organising staff in continuing professional development (CPD) trios. This meant that the lesson was observed by two members of staff (mentor and another teacher) and a university tutor, plus a stationary tripod-mounted camera! During her lesson, the learning of nine students (from a class of 28) was observed and recorded in annotations on the lesson plan. The evaluation meeting focused on the experiences and responses of the nine students, giving detailed feedback on the impact of each stage of the lesson and these students' level of engagement. The mentor believed that the student-teacher's teaching changed significantly afterwards and became much more confident. Her subsequent focus for development was use of differentiation and the mentor reported:

She started thinking: how can I get all the kids engaged? ... There was a huge change.

In subsequent 'unobserved' lessons, student-teacher 'E' reported that she thought about how to achieve a stronger focus on learning. Building on the experience of having the learning observed in her research lessons, she introduced systematic 'buddy learning checks', a form of collaborative peer assessment that involved her students collaboratively reviewing one another's learning. Her experienced geography mentor advised that E's confidence grew following the observed research lesson (the middle one of three) in ways that would normally take longer, and he believed that her rate of development in the first teaching practice outstripped that of student-teachers he had worked with in the traditional mode:

> *Things that would normally take a long time ... suddenly they just accelerated after that observed lesson and the feedback she got...*

Her lesson planning became more efficient and instead of working until very early in the morning, the student-teacher was completing preparation by 9 or 10 pm. Such commentaries suggest that the construction of learning becomes clearer to student teachers involved in lesson studies, as a result of collaborative planning and evaluation of how plans relate to the action of learning in classrooms.

The mentor believed that he had been inducted into '*a whole new way of looking at guiding student-teachers*' and was so enthused that he took the process to his next departmental meeting:

> *This is a whole new thing ... I went to a departmental meeting. I am going to try this in my department.*

He described how the department (seven teachers) reviewed planning for a Year 7 lesson in the light of his experience of LS with the student-teacher. In addition, his department intends to use LS to prepare the ground for the new geography curriculum in 2014.

Making the link between planning and the physical act of teaching (through the observation), and participating in the collaborative evaluation, enable student-teachers to get to grips with the whole cycle of pedagogic endeavour with a more experienced colleague. This cycle involves thinking about learners, mediating the syllabus, planning, teaching and evaluating in a supportive and supported context of collaboration. This not only permits student-teachers to move more rapidly towards the centre of the community of practice, both conceptually and linguistically, but also opens up the complexity of the pedagogic process to detailed critical scrutiny, resulting in greater understanding and confidence. Consequently, the student-teacher is less reliant on 'trial-and-error' approaches to development as often happens in school placements.

This, we believe, is the principal achievement of LS in ITE, the detailed and collaborative opportunity to explore *the complex system of classroom-oriented processes*, what we identify as the 'pedagogic black-box'. This box can remain partially or even wholly shut in individually-oriented teacher placements but is unlocked and opened for investigation by the focused collaboration of the community of teachers (expert and novice) in lesson studies. Our argument in support of LS as the key to opening the 'pedagogic black box' is set out in the next section.

Opening the pedagogic black box in ITE

Through LS, the student teacher and mentor collaborate in a consistent dialogue about pedagogy. The student-teacher is not only afforded the opportunity to engage with the thought processes of a more experienced colleague, but is also encouraged to offer suggestions, leading to a legitimate and active input into the development of the pedagogy for research lessons.

This contrasts with traditional models of ITE, such as that in England, which is based on partnerships between schools and universities with a natural division of focus and labour. The university partner becomes responsible for introducing aspects of educational theory, and also for developing initial pedagogic models for use in school placements. The school partners, who host student-teachers for their eight-week placements, utilise theory by embedding what has been learned in the university phase of training in an emergent and developing set of practical skills. This leads to school placements focusing on developing understanding and practical application of pedagogy as a set of competences within the classroom. This common division of labour in school–university partnership can lead to a linear model of learning. Early exposure to educational ideas is built upon through close work with the school-based mentor. Student-teachers plan a lesson, the teaching of which is observed, leading to *ex post facto* suggestions for improvement. In some cases, this is forestalled by the student-teacher being asked to submit lesson plans in advance for scrutiny, amendment and/or approval. The student-teacher interprets mentor feedback, enacting their suggestions to the best of their ability. Observation of their teaching checks that student-teachers' interpretation of the feedback was correct. In this way, student-teachers act as 'apprentices', interpreting and acting upon the 'pearls of wisdom' offered by their mentors. Here, there is slow accretion of understanding and expertise based on a 'trial-and-error' model of learning in which student-teacher learning is developed little by little.

The inclusion of LS within ITE brings a very different approach to the development of student-teachers. Whereas the 'dominant model' of ITE sees the developing understanding and application of pedagogy as linear, LS introduces a critical-holistic model which deliberately opens up the process of pedagogy in its entirety from planning, to teaching, to evaluation with mentors and student-teachers collaboratively co-constructing the process together.

This collaboration builds on the practical foundation and theoretical basis of the work completed within the university. Rather than gaining glimpses of the complexity of pedagogy over many weeks, LS confronts the complexity of teaching and learning early in the teaching placement as mentor and student-teacher develop and evaluate a research lesson as partners. Furthermore, the student-teacher has the opportunity to understand how the thought processes that contribute to planning relate to the actuality of the lesson through observation of the mentor teaching the first jointly planned lesson. Subsequent to this, collaborative evaluation allows for further explicit discussion of pedagogy, before the student-teacher undertakes the lesson with a different group of pupils. As a result, the student-teacher and mentor engage in close consideration of pedagogy through collaborative planning, observation and evaluation.

Following two teaching practices in which he used lesson study with two geography student-teachers, an experienced mentor felt that the process enabled the student-teachers to be more fully engaged as members of the department. In discussion with the university tutor and the second of his student-teachers (H), the mentor described the effects of the mutuality that is inherent to LS:

> *It's that feeling of 'you're not a student, you're actually a member of the department'. Your advice is as important as anyone else's. I actually respect what you've got to say because you actually see things in observations that I don't because I'm thinking of other things like OfSTED progress ... What it does is it allows me to use your eyes and your interviewing [of case students]. ... I need to depend on you [observing].*

Such detailed collaboration leads to a much more explicit consideration of pedagogy between mentor and student-teacher early in a placement, leading to deeper understanding of the inherent complexity of the classroom and the complex nature of learning and teaching. In this way, LS opens up the 'pedagogic black box' from the start of the training process leading to a more holistic development processes. The collaborative and predictive nature of the process can be seen in the following words of a student teacher of geography as he contrasts the discursive approach of LS with individualistic planning which is often the hallmark of ITE work:

> *You're discussing it so ... aren't you? So you know exactly what should be coming out of the lesson, not what is coming out of your lesson because of what you have decided to teach.*
>
> (Geography student-teacher 'H')

The approach is informed by and focused on the development of 'embedded' and linked elements of pedagogy. In this way, LS is a process which opens up the 'pedagogic black box', identifying and discussing pedagogy as a complex, emergent, holistic set of processes, better understood through in-depth and intensive discussion between mentor and student-teacher.

Implications for ITE in school-based programmes

We have introduced LS into our postgraduate teacher education programme at a time of great change in the system. In future years, student-teachers will gain the vast majority of their pedagogic insights from school-based mentors. As we write, teaching alliances are being forged with federations of schools to offer teacher training places. These involve universities, but their role is no longer one of leadership. In England, a number of employment-based routes into teaching are becoming more widespread and present a significant challenge to the traditional university-led provision. This rapidly evolving and diverse provision includes the salaried School Direct Training Programme, in which student-teachers are employed as unqualified teachers, and Teach First, a two-year employment-based training route in which student-teachers are paid for the first year as unqualified teachers and follow a two-year Leadership Development Programme.

The Teach First programme includes a Post-graduate Certificate of Education and, in the second year, participants are paid as newly qualified teachers.

Fee-paying routes into teaching remain but, as suggested above, will be increasingly school-led, such as for example School Direct for which student-teachers spend most of their time in a school where they have the opportunity to teach lessons and learn from experienced teachers. An alternative is School-Centred Initial Teacher Training (SCITT) which is a one-year full-time programme offered by schools and colleges stressing practical, hands-on experience. In both cases, input from higher education partners plays a role as most courses value the masters-level input to training programmes and have included masters-level modules in their specifications.

We argue that the exploration of pedagogy in supported, developmental ways will surely have to remain at the heart of all such programmes unless we wish to move to an exclusively craft model of teacher education in which new entrants simply imitate the experienced. The role of the mentor as the bridge between pedagogic theory and practice will become even more crucial to the success of ITE. Offering LS along the lines that we have developed could provide one formative way of inducting new teachers not only into how to teach but also into how to learn to teach (Hiebert *et al.*, 2003). This will provide a platform not only for the development of competences (meeting national standards, for example DfE, 2012) that will enable participants to achieve qualified teacher status but also prepare them for a career in which continual enquiry and learning are an expectation of their professional engagement.

As teacher education programmes evolve in this direction, the role of universities will change as they act as partners with schools to provide inputs on pedagogic theory and research, but also support schools to develop enquiry-oriented approaches to teacher development. We would argue that LS provides one optimal approach to supporting teacher education not only in relation to pedagogic skills but also in relation to the development of classroom enquiry that will prepare teachers for continual learning. It is unrealistic to believe that school-based programmes will necessarily equip teachers with 'the finished competencies of effective teaching' (Hiebert *et al.*, 2003: 202). Effective teaching requires continual engagement in classroom enquiry. Our studies suggest that LS, conducted with experienced school-based colleagues and supported by university teachers, is a rich way of helping new teachers to explore and develop their pedagogy. In addition LS is at its most potent when experienced and critically engaged mentors support the growth in student-teachers' pedagogic understanding and practice; in turn this requires the quality of pedagogic thinking and practice of mentors to be very well developed, open to change and new ideas.

Conclusion

Such was the confidence expressed by both mentors and student-teachers in our case studies that we are confident that the model we propose has the flexibility and rigour to support both student-teacher and mentor development. Our field-testing of LS from a Community of Practice perspective reveals clear benefits with student-teachers more fully integrated into departmental teams than has been our experience with the traditional model. LS offers a collaborative complement to the traditional approach of teaching placements, in which the student-teacher plans and teaches lessons as an individual, with periodic support from the mentor. Of course, some student-teachers develop quickly in this environment but our experience suggests that integrating LS enriches the learning of both participants by providing a focal initiative for the collaborative understanding and development of pedagogy. Crucially, participants share an approach to developing expertise that is founded on collaborative consideration of learning, an understanding and implementation of the art of planning, and engagement in collaborative evaluation and reflection. Thus, LS provides not only support for student-teachers to learn how to learn to teach (Hiebert *et al.*, 2003: 202) but also professional development for mentors.

Use of LS in ITE is in its infancy and further studies are needed to assess its impact and evaluate the extent to which models like ours can bridge the theory–practice divide as ITE becomes ever more school-led. Furthermore, our focus was predominantly located in the interactive dimension of the learning process. However, Illeris (2007) argues that the act of learning is composed of three inter-related dimensions (the individual, the emotional and the social); the social can be interrogated through the interaction of those involved, as we have done in our exploration of LS. By focusing solely on the social aspect of the process, it is possible to lose sight of the individual agency involved in the professional learning of student-teachers and mentors. The individual and the emotional are important lenses through which learning needs to be understood, but are more difficult to capture and analyse.

Therefore, other evaluative approaches are needed, which embrace a more nuanced complex analysis of professional learning through LS. Meanwhile, we will pursue this agenda with greater use of LS in teaching placements.

Acknowledgement

We are very grateful to the mentors, collaborating teachers and student-teachers who participated in this pilot. This chapter has been written with the support of a small research grant from the Society for Educational Studies and study leave from the University of Leicester.

References

Ben-Peretz, M. (2001). The Impossible Role of Teacher Educators in a Changing World. *Journal of Teacher Education*, 52(1): 48–56.

Carrier S.J. (2011). Implementing and Integrating Effective Teaching Strategies Including Features of Lesson Study in an Elementary Science Methods Course. *The Teacher Educator*, 46(2): 145–60.

Cavey, L.O. and Berenson, S.B. (2005). Learning to teach high school mathematics: Patterns of growth in understanding right triangle trigonometry during lesson-plan study. *Journal of Mathematical Behaviour*, 24: 171–90.

Chassels, C. and Melville W. (2009). Collaborative, Reflective, and Iterative Japanese Lesson Study in an Initial Teacher Education Program: Benefits and Challenges. *Canadian Journal of Education*, 32(4): 734–63.

Cohan A. and Honigsfeld A. (2007). Incorporating 'Lesson Study' in Teacher Preparation. *The Educational Forum*, 71(1): 81–92.

Davies, P. and Dunnill, R. (2008). Learning Study as a Model of Collaborative Practice in Initial Teacher Education. *Journal of Education for Teaching: International Research and Pedagogy*, 34(1): 3–16.

Department for Children, Schools and Families, DCSF (2008). *Improving practice and progression through lesson study*. London: DCSF. http://webarchive. nationalarchives.gov.uk/20110202093118/http:/nationalstrategies.standards. dcsf.gov.uk/node/132730 (Accessed 20 January 2012).

Department for Education, DfE (2012). *Teaching Standards*. London: DfE. http://webarchive.nationalarchives.gov.uk/20130401151715/https://www. education.gov.uk/publications/eOrderingDownload/teachers%20standards. pdf (Accessed 20 June 2013).

Dudley, P. (2011). *Lesson Study: a handbook*. Cambridge: LSUK. http://lesson-study.co.uk/wp-content/uploads/2012/03/Lesson_Study_Handbook_-_011011-1. pdf (Accessed 20 January 2012).

Farrell, T.S.C. (2006). The first year of language teaching: imposing order. *System*, 34(2): 211–21.

Fernandez, M.L. (2005). Learning through Microteaching Lesson Study in Teacher Preparation. *Action in Teacher Education*, 26(4): 37–47.

Fernandez, M.L. (2010). Investigating How and What Prospective Teachers Learn through Microteaching Lesson Study. *Teaching and Teacher Education*, 26(2): 351–62.

Galanouli, D. (2010). *School-Based Professional Development*. Belfast: General Teaching Council for Northern Ireland.

Gurl, T. (2010). Improving Preservice Field Placements in Secondary Mathematics: A Residency Model for Student Teaching through Lesson Study. *Journal of Mathematics Education at Teachers College*, 1(1): 17–20.

Gurl, T. (2011). A model for incorporating lesson study into the student teaching placement: what worked and what did not? *Educational Studies*, 37(5): 523–8.

Hardman, M.L. (2009). Redesigning the preparation of all teachers within the framework of an integrated program model. *Teaching and Teacher Education*, 25(4): 583–7.

Hiebert, J., Morris A. and Glass, B. (2003). Learning to Learn to Teach: An 'Experiment' Model for Teaching and Teacher Preparation in Mathematics. *Journal of Mathematics Teacher Education*, 6(2): 201–22.

Hobson, A.J., Ashby P., Malderez, A. and Tomlinson P.D. (2009). Mentoring beginning teachers: What we know and what we don't. *Teaching and Teacher Education*, 25: 207–16.

Illeris, K. (2007). *How We Learn: Learning and Non-Learning in School and Beyond*. London: Taylor and Francis.

Kotelawala, U. (2012). Lesson Study in a Methods Course: Connecting Teacher Education to the Field. *Teacher Educator*, 47(1): 67–89.

Leavy, A.M. (2010). The Challenge of Preparing Preservice Teachers to Teach Informal Inferential Reasoning. *Statistics Education Research Journal*, 9(1): 46–67.

Marble, S.T. (2006). Learning to Teach through Lesson Study. *Action in Teacher Education*, 28(3): 86–96.

Marble, S.T. (2007). Inquiring into Teaching: Lesson Study in Elementary Science Methods. *Journal of Science Teacher Education*, 18(6): 935–53.

McMahon, M.T. and Hines, E. (2008). Lesson Study with Preservice Teachers. *Mathematics Teacher*, 102(3): 186–91.

Myers, J. (2012). Lesson Study as a Means for Facilitating Preservice Teacher Reflectivity. *International Journal for the Scholarship of Teaching and Learning*, 6(1): 1–21. http://www.georgiasouthern.edu/ijsotl (Accessed 12 December 2012).

Pang, M.F. and Ling, L.M. (2012). Learning study: helping teachers to use theory, develop professionally, and produce new knowledge to be shared. *Instructional Science*, 40: 589–606.

Parks, A.N. (2008). Messy learning: Preservice teachers' lesson-study conversations about mathematics and students. *Teaching and Teacher Education*, 24: 1200–16.

Parks, A.N. (2009). Collaborating about what? An instructor's look at preservice lesson study. *Teacher Education Quarterly*, 36(4): 81–97.

Powney, J. and Watts, M. (1987). *Interviewing in Educational Research*. London: Routledge and Kegan Paul.

Ricks, T.E. (2011). Process Reflection during Japanese Lesson Study Experiences by Prospective Secondary Mathematics Teachers. *Journal of Mathematics Teacher Education*, 14(4): 251–67.

Rock, T.C. (2003). A Lesson Study Model for Preservice Teacher Education. *Journal of Research in Education*, 13(1): 31–8.

Sims, L. and Walsh, D. (2009). Lesson Study with Preservice Teachers: Lessons from Lessons. *Teaching and Teacher Education*, 25(5): 724–33.

Teaching Agency (2012). *The Newly Qualified Teacher Survey*. London: Teaching Agency. http://www.education.gov.uk/schools/careers/traininganddevelopment/a00200667/nqt-survey (Accessed 12 March 2013).

Tsui, A.B.M. and Law, D.Y.K. (2007). Learning as boundary crossing in school–university partnership. *Teaching and Teacher Education*, 23: 1289–301.

Wenger, E. (1998). *Communities of Practice: Learning, Meaning, and Identity*. Cambridge: Cambridge University Press.

Wenger, E. (2000). Communities of Practice and Social Learning Systems. *Organization*, 7(2): 225–46.

Chapter 6

Evolving the curriculum through Lesson Study in Japan

Hiroyuki Kuno

'The 21st Century is the age of the knowledge-society'. So says the introduction to every copy of the *Heisei 20 Japanese National Curriculum* launched in 2008. It continues: '...in which new knowledge, information and technology grow in value in every social field including politics, economics and culture' (MEXT, 2008: 1).

In this Chapter I examine how the Japanese curriculum has in fact constantly changed and evolved over time and how Lesson Study (LS) plays a critical role in that process.

I will contrast this with the ways in which some other countries develop their national curricula, and as a result of these contrasts I will argue that there should be a role for LS not only in improving the *practice* of teaching and in improving pupils' learning (which is how people in the UK typically tend to view and use LS), but importantly also that LS should have a role in enabling school curricula as well as local and national curricula to develop more *scientifically* than is typically the case in the West. The scientific approach which I advocate, and which has LS at its heart, enables these school, local and national levels of the curriculum to be simultaneously rooted-in, stemming from the knowledge of the content that we want children to learn but equally, and also importantly, from our knowledge about *how children most successfully learn this curriculum content*. In Japan both of these sets of knowledge inform the curriculum that we design for our children and the way we teach it to them (Kuno 2006, 2011).

As well as pointing out the needs of a knowledge society, the 1998 *Heisei 10 Japanese National Curriculum* overview also set out some very familiar curricular goals, the like of which you are likely to find somewhere in the national curriculum literature of many countries (Ministry of Education, Science and Culture, 1998). These goals include: the promotion of reading, literacy and communication; enhanced mathematics and science education; practical hands-on learning, and also

new content such as the development of 'thinking skills' and the introduction of foreign language activities in elementary schools that can also
be found in England's almost contemporary 'Curriculum 2000' (Hodgson
and Spours, 2003). Countries introduced skills like these at the turn of
the century with an eye to globalisation and the communication skills
and knowledge needed for a country to succeed in an international
knowledge society (Kuno and Watanabe, 2009).

These ideas have subsequently been developed further in Japan.
The 2008 *Heisei 20 Japanese National Curriculum* builds upon these
developments with the introduction of what it terms 'the 21st Century
competencies'. And again, if we look at the development of curricula
internationally, there is a common focus on the development of similar
'21st Century competencies' (Dede, 2007, 2009). You will find it echoed
in suggestions put forward by the Partnership for 21st Century Skills
(2006), the OECD (Ananiadou and Claro, 2009; OECD, 2011; Schleicher,
2012), enGauge 21st Century Skills (Metiri Group and NCREL, 2003)
and the American Association of Colleges and Universities (2007). All
these have tended to describe competencies that include:

- Information and communications technology (ICT) skills;
- Thinking skills (including critical thinking and creative thinking);
- Linguistic communication (including foreign languages);
- Social dimensions including the global mindset and civic literacy;
- Interaction, collaboration and cooperation skills including
  leadership.

In the West one can find evidence that this has been something that
schools themselves have developed autonomously (where their national
curriculum legislation or accountability systems have provided them
the space to do so.) Finnish educators such as Aho have documented
how, in recent years, schools in Finland have used the *school curriculum* to create a curricular experience for their learners which is not
based upon recitation, student recording or 'seat-based learning' but
which instead has 'gradually been transformed into more flexible, open
and interaction-rich environments where an active role for students
comes first' (Aho *et al.*, 2006: 14).

Desforges considers how schools in England might respond to the
emphasis in England's 2014 National Curriculum, which follows in
Finland's footsteps, by having a school-designed element of the curriculum. Desforges proposes that the school curriculum might promote

the skills and attributes that are most associated with 'expert learners' to help students to become more expert in learning and thus more independent and resilient in organising their studies and development through later life. These skills are:

- the will to learn;
- the ability to form learning objectives (they are self-challenging);
- persistence in adversity;
- knowledge of learning processes;
- basic skills;
- creativity and flexibility (Desforges, 2012: 3).

This chapter will initially take a school-level focus and examine how LS plays a role in shaping the evolution of the school curriculum in one Japanese school as it sought to integrate these twenty-first-century learning demands with the range of traditional curricular demands, in order to create an integrated curriculum experience that is coherent, relevant, deep and motivating for its pupils as a result. I will propose that this rich, motivating and relevant pupil experience can only be achieved and sustained by the active, simultaneous study of pupils' learning in this curriculum in order that the curricular and pedagogical approaches can be fine tuned to meet the particular needs of different classes and pupils as they learn and develop (Sato *et al.*, 2009).

I then go on to take a whole system view and argue that this linkage between knowledge of the curricular content and knowledge of how children learn it best helps the Japanese school curriculum to act as a springboard into wider, deeper and more independent and collaborative learning for students – beyond school and beyond self. But I will demonstrate also that for this to work effectively the school system is required to be constantly alert to the knowledge about pupil learning that is being discovered on a daily basis through lesson studies across its schools.

Integrated Studies and Lesson Study working together in the Japanese school curriculum

The 1998 Heisei 10 Japanese National Curriculum Integrated Studies defined pathways for children to learn how to develop and how to put into action approaches to solving multi-faceted topical problems. The aim is for them to be able to do this together, collaboratively, so that they are prepared for dealing with complex social issues later as they go through their lives.

They learn to:

i   turn their eyes to a variety of 'issues' current in their local community or country or in the wider world;

ii   set themselves challenges relating to these issues;

iii   seek out, explore and research a range of data and information – including statistical data and web content that can provide them with a broader understanding of the issue and how it is viewed by people with a variety of different opinions;

iv   seek the views and experiences of people such as experts and community leaders in order to gain deeper insights into the issue;

v   exchange views, ideas and opinions with a range of people from both within and beyond school, using oral and web-based means;

vi   look deeply into what they find by applying these steps (ii–v above) recursively in order to create greater depth and definition in their views as well as to seek out and explore their own insights into the issues

vii   take carefully planned, concerted action *in real life* in order to help to solve the problem or to resolve the issue.

Thus, since the beginning of this century, children across Japan have utilised this problem-solving enquiry process (known in Japanese as '*Tankyu*') to take on and to intelligently tackle real issues that they identify in the world at large.

The National Curriculum requires each school to design and publish goals and contents for its own school curriculum and to present this as a Scheme of Work that is based on the primary objectives of the Integrated Studies element of the school curriculum listed above.

Unlike the subjects of the Japanese National Curriculum, the goals and content of the integrated curriculum (beyond the broad outcomes specified above) are entirely the school's choice and the expectation is that the teachers in schools should be competent to design and to teach the Integrated Studies element of the school curriculum based upon their knowledge and understanding of their pupils, their pupils' needs and the demands that are placed upon them at home, locally in the community and nationally in the world beyond school.

All this forms the basis for Integrated Studies in the Japanese curriculum and it clearly places a new set of demands upon students. This curriculum could certainly no longer be described as 'systematised individual knowledge' but like many countries that have developed their curricula beyond the recommendations of PISA 2000's 'competency blueprint for problem solving', the Japanese integrated curriculum places these new demands not only upon students but on their teachers and schools (Kuno, 2013: 158).

In the following section I will illustrate how LS can offer a means by which these new, integrated competencies can be developed simultaneously by students, teachers and, organisationally, by their schools.

How Lesson Study helps with curriculum design, revision and implementation

For Japanese teachers who have grown up with lesson studies being conducted when they were pupils themselves, and with LS as a key aspect of their own professional learning from their initial training until their retirement, there was no difficulty in seeing the connections between LS and curriculum revision. It was a natural assumption.

This is not only because LS is so deeply ingrained in Japanese teachers' professional subconscious as a process. It is also because there are two important commonalities between processes of LS and processes of curriculum revision. Both centre on i) enquiry that is designed to examine the way content, pedagogy and learning interact and ii) both have the potential to support collaborative teacher learning that can result in improved practice and future learning design that is tailored to pupil needs. I will now elaborate on this further.

I) COMMON ENQUIRY FOCUS

Both curriculum revision and LS involve a critical development cycle that is found in action research in the West and which is often referred to as 'Plan, Do, Review' or in Japan as PDCA (Plan-Do-Check-Action). LS involves the joint preparation of a draft teaching plan, carrying out research lessons, reviewing and analysing the learning that took place in post-lesson discussions and the reflecting on what was discovered and adjusting subsequent teaching in order to take-on this new knowledge. In the UK we tend to think of lesson studies as leading to pedagogical adjustments, but if one blurs the distinction between curriculum content and pedagogy, it is clear that this approach can form the basis for a deeply focused review of the impact of curriculum content and design on pupil learning.

Shulman's (1986) work in the US has helped to map out the 'blurred' area between curriculum content and pedagogy. He describes aspects of curriculum knowledge which go far beyond 'subject knowledge' and he calls them 'Pedagogical Content Knowledge' (PCK). PCK is the knowledge a teacher needs to possess, not only about the aspect of the subject he or she is teaching but also about how it relates to all the other associated aspects and concepts and what common misconceptions pupils form when they are learning this particular content. (Examples of how LS develops PCK are described in detail in the first chapter of this book.) Lesson studies can be carried out systematically in order to examine the ways in which an aspect of curriculum design may help or hinder pupils' learning or teachers' teaching. It allows teachers to investigate the extent to which the curriculum design is allowing teachers to develop and to utilise PCK effectively in order to support pupils' learning successfully.

II) THE POTENTIAL TO BUILD LEARNING COMMUNITIES CAPABLE OF IMPROVING THE RELATIONSHIP BETWEEN CURRICULUM CONTENT, CURRICULUM DESIGN AND PEDAGOGICAL PRACTICE IN ORDER TO IMPROVE PUPIL LEARNING

It is widely accepted that teachers need to hold their practice-knowledge both consciously in their heads and tacitly in their subconscious. This is in order to cope with the complexities and pace of a class of 30 children all attempting to master new knowledge at once (see Chapter 1). Such swift complexity, coupled with the mix of conscious and subconscious knowledge being used at once, restricts the abilities of teachers to share that knowledge with each other (Dudley, 2013). This makes it difficult for teachers to be aware of much of the professional knowledge they possess and use in day-to-day practice.

Collaborative, discursive learning in groups allows them to harness the powers of the 'learning community' (Wenger *et al.*, 2002) and the power of learning through talk (Mercer, 1995) in order to able to see and act upon aspects of their professional knowledge that are invisible to them and to have the confidence in the relationships of the 'community' to take risks and to try out new ideas.

Thus teachers' practice knowledge can be described as 'sticky practice knowledge' (Brown and Duguid, 2002) which is so hard to mobilise and transfer. But much the same can be said in relation to the effects of curriculum structure and design upon pupil learning. If it is hard for teachers to see and understand their practice then it is hard for them to see and to understand how the curriculum affects their practice and affects in turn the learning of their pupils. LS's properties of making learning more visible to teachers and providing a professional community context in which teachers feel that it is safe to analyse and explore these practices also makes it possible for them to examine effects of the curriculum on their pupils' learning and to redesign and revise it accordingly where this is necessary.

All this is particularly important for the design and development of the Integrated Studies elements of the school curriculum because it is teachers themselves who are responsible for the design and development of this part of the curriculum. Continual critical examination of the effects of Integrated Studies on pupil learning helps teachers in Japan to make decisions as informed professionals based upon the best possible information available to them which emanates from their systematic lesson studies. As such they are operating 'in praxis' (Schön, 1983). And it is teachers who have to establish a quality and competency scheme to help them to map out the progress and achievements that their pupils will make as a result of their experience of nine years (six in elementary and three in middle school) of integrated study.

Developing a quality and competency framework through lesson studies for an Integrated Studies curriculum in Kuchiyokawa elementary school, Miki City, Japan

In this section I describe how this process took place at Kuchiyokawa elementary school. Kuchiyokawa was selected by the Ministry of Education, Culture, Sports, Science and Technology as a National Research School. This was on the grounds of the high quality of education it provides and as a result of the quality of its LS practice in driving continual improvement in that quality.

The teachers at Kuchiyokawa designed their school curriculum for Integrated Studies based on the qualities and competencies listed above. The six dimensions were chosen to reflect the aims of this aspect of the devolved national curriculum, the interests that children have shown in activities that address some of these dimensions and themes in the past, but also with the intention of creating real-life situations and contexts for children to learn in the community by interacting with members of the community (Kuchiyokawa Kindergarten and Primary School, 2003, 2005).

Table 6.1 Dimensions for the Minagino Integrated Studies course

Dimensions	Contents
Life and Health	Learning about life and care of human beings and livings things
Growth and Self	Learning about our development and careers in our future
Living inventions and safety	Learning about inventions for daily life and own safety in school and kindergarten
Co-existence	Learning about how people co-exist in society as well as understanding international relations, and welfare
Local community	Learning about people's way of life and situations, problems and co-operation in our local community around school
Natural environment	Learning about desirable nature and environment in relation with local people around school

The six dimensions and their contents can be seen in Table 6.1.

The characteristics of these integrated curricular dimensions reflect the fact that this integrated element of the school curriculum is designed for use with children in pre-school settings and in lower grades in elementary schools broadly corresponding to the Foundation Stage and Key Stage 1 in schools in England.

Thus it incorporates aspects of 'discovery of knowledge through play', and the development of stages of self-awareness which are familiar aspects of Early Years child development and learning. It also embraces aspects of the Japanese formal National Curriculum, which seem to fit well within these integrated studies. These include aspects of dimensions such as 'International Understanding', 'Environment' and 'Health and Wellbeing'. These strands were woven-in, deftly integrated into the school curriculum.

It is important to note also, that all these strands can be traced developing in complexity and demand from year to year as children develop and can cope with more complex, challenging and multi-faceted situations that arise in real life.

The teachers at Kuchiyokawa mapped this progression into greater levels of complexity and challenge through the use of competencies. Strands of competencies that describe the developing integrated complexities of the learning outcomes children achieve were arranged into what they term a 'Competency Catalogue' for their Integrated Studies scheme of work. These competencies escalate in demand, complexity and levels of integration as can be seen in Table 6.2 which lists the examples from

Table 6.2 Escalating Competency Descriptors for the Natural Environment Integrated Studies strands

Dimension	Natural Environment
Goal	Realising and understanding the importance of having a rich, natural and built environment in the locality
Content	
Kindergarten	a **Emotional aspect**: to appreciate the scale, beauty, mystery and significance of familiar natural things in everyday life b **Cognitive aspect** c **Aspect for social participation**
Grades 1 and 2	a **Emotional aspect**: to comprehend the scale, beauty and mystery and significance of familiar natural things in everyday life and to discover a love of nature and the local environment b **Cognitive aspect** c **Aspect for social participation**
Grades 3 and 4	a **Emotional aspect**: to actively get involved with different local areas of natural environment and learn how nature provides us with rich and varied benefits b **Cognitive aspect** c **Aspect for social participation**
Grades 5 and 6	a **Emotional aspect**: to enhance sensitivity, develop interests and cultivate the mind in order to love and care for nature b **Cognitive aspect** c **Aspect for social participation**

the aspect of the catalogue relating to the emotional aspects of learning to be developed in the 'Natural Environment' dimension.

In summary then, the overall outcome of this natural environment dimension is that pupils will have developed understanding of and have formed a love for nature in their local surroundings in a manner that promotes coexistence. This will have nurtured pupils' competency in finding creative and resourceful ways of preserving the natural environment in sustainable ways and of enhancing it still further.

As can be seen in Table 6.2, this dimension strand develops through three strands of development: a) the emotional aspect, which develops care and love for nature and the environment; b) the cognitive aspect, which develops knowledge and awareness of the environment; and c) the aspect for social participation, which develops pupils' own interactions with nature and the environment and those which they engage in with others.

Table 6.2 provides a detailed illustration of how the first of these strands – the emotional aspect – develops pupils as they themselves develop and learn. The adjectives and verbs trace out the deepening quality of the learning that is expected of pupils. In the earlier years they are realising, then appreciating, then comprehending, then getting actively involved with and finally 'enhancing sensitivity' and 'cultivating their minds'. In earlier years they are developing these in order to realise 'importance'. But this develops into 'scale, beauty, mystery and significance' leading to the discovery of 'love' for nature which later stimulates pupils when they are older still, to 'care for, preserve and sustainably enhance' the local natural environment.

What sets these sequences of curricular development apart from many similar sequences in curricular literature or textbooks, is that these sequences were distilled and crystallised by teachers from repeated analyses of how their pupils, over successive years, had learned in these strands and the identification of the ways of learning that had most enhanced pupils' knowledge, beliefs and values. This was achieved through their analysis of years of LS data. They initially used these data to inform the design and construction of rough frames upon which to structure the competency strands. They then worked through a two-day process of structured analytical discussion, again informed by their LS data. The section that follows describes that process of analysis.

The methodology through which teachers at Kuchiyokawa designed this Integrated Studies curriculum based upon knowledge of how pupils had learned most successfully in these areas of the curriculum

The first stage of this workshop involved teachers working in groups, analysing their data from previous observations and lesson studies carried out in these areas. The product of these discussions was a collection of over 200 memos about the most valuable aspects of children's motivation, learning, progress and overcoming of barriers that had been observed in recent years. These are called 'Learning moments for children' and each memo was labelled with the academic year group, subject, and activity name along with a brief description of the learning moment and its qualities. They were classified according to the six dimensions and the stages of development or academic years they best fitted.

For example, one memo from a research lesson recorded how impressive it had been to observe the levels of motivation experienced by pupils in talking to and taking care of ducks. Another recorded how they had gained knowledge by making very high quality observations and descriptions of ducks' 'quack tones' and another of the learning moments observed the result on pupil learning of recordings and observations pupils had made of the way that the ducks' feathers grew and changed over time.

In the second stage of the discussion, groups of teachers abstracted from these collections of concrete examples of learning moments a means to describe the broader achievement goals to which these collections of learning moments had most contributed. The aim of the discussion was to use the escalating strands of qualities and competencies to agree what the children had learned from the range of activities discussed that had generated such powerful learning moments. Once arranged across the qualities and competencies, the curriculum could then be trialed in practice.

In conclusion then, this has been an account of how teachers developed an integrated curriculum from evidence of successful pupil learning and the practices that brought about that successful learning. Through structured discussion, teachers brought together and pooled the knowledge they had gathered over years of research lessons about activities that had produced key learning moments for pupils. They used their research lesson reviews as the prime source of evidence for these discussions. They then categorised and re-categorised these learning moments until they had created, from the specific activities, more abstract, generalised curriculum pathways which could then be used by teachers to plan, teach and to begin to assess Grade 2 pupils' learning in their new integrated school curriculum for Life and Health.

Using Lesson Study approaches to evaluate and improve the integrated curriculum as it is taught

The next stage in this account focuses on how Japanese teachers use LS processes to evaluate how well the curriculum they have created is serving its purpose of helping teachers to create the kinds of learning moments for children that will replicate the very best of those learning moments that contributed to its design.

Teachers at Kuchiyokawa spent the following year carefully:

- analysing and revising their schemes of work in order to accommodate the new curriculum content;
- revising their teaching plans so that the lessons and teaching sequences used to deliver this part of the integrated school curriculum faithfully reflect the aims and ambitions of the new scheme of work. In addition to the identification of any gaps in the teaching plan, teachers also review and revise the teaching materials, learning strategies, resources and contexts that are to be used to teach this element of the scheme of work;
- carrying out regular research lessons and reviewing the evidence obtained of pupil learning and behaviours in order to help them to judge the extent to which the curriculum is successfully creating the kinds of learning outcomes that they had so carefully planned.

The school published a comprehensive report at the end of the year. This detailed precisely which areas of the new integrated curriculum had not created the kinds of learning anticipated and provided records of the revisions and redesigns that had been constructed and trialed in order to achieve the learning that was originally envisaged when the curriculum was first planned the previous year. Despite the careful planning of this integrated curriculum and the fact that it was founded upon examples of successful pupil learning in these curriculum areas, the school had made considerable revisions to its integrated school curriculum by the end of the first year of teaching it. Revisions were made to the following dimensions: 'Life and Health; Inventions and safety in play and life; 'Co-existence'; Community life' and 'Natural environment'. In some dimensions up to a third of the curriculum was re-designed as a result of this initial strategic LS-based evaluation.

In order to bring this to life for the reader, I will now give a detailed account of the changes that were made in the integrated curriculum dimension of 'Growth and Self' at Kuchiyokawa, using lesson studies to refine and adapt the curriculum for 'Growth and Self'.

The design process based on reviews of lesson studies (described above) had led the school to reject its original plan which had been for children to measure their physical fitness and from these measurements to extrapolate learning about not only their physical health but also about their personal, moral and social development as individuals. Further review and discussion took place from which emerged a more elaborate plan which was to bring either school 'alumni' or key community figures who have taken advantage of talents they have in relation to health or fitness or sport to develop these talents and skills but, in addition, to broaden these aspects of physical prowess and expertise into their lives more generally. This was planned so as to create a stimulating introduction to the unit.

The first trial of this revised approach led the school to invite a local community figure – Mr Tomoya Kiuchi – into the school to talk to the Grade 6 pupils. At the time, Mr Kiuchi was world 'skipping rope' champion. This was planned also to be the first research lesson of this evaluative cycle. Mr Kiuchi proved to be a 'hit' with pupils. He shared many of his skipping techniques with them after giving an initial talk in which he told the story of how he had dreamed, strived and finally succeeded in becoming a champion – and eventually the world champion. He tutored students in how to use many of his techniques during his talk.

The research lesson observation data record how captivated children were by his talk and by his determination to achieve his goal. They were clearly also applying lessons they had learned from listening to him, to their views of their own lives to come. These are some of their words recorded by observers during the research lesson.

What struck my heart most strongly is that it is important to keep working, and studying at school and not to be discouraged by set-backs – but to carry on.

He said to me 'Are you doing road races? Do you attend school every day? Don't give up on what you are doing now – I support you.' I was glad to hear that I was very moved by his words because it is such a rare opportunity to meet someone like him.

He did not give up anything until he was 23 years old. So he only earned his world champion title after a 13-year challenge. I want to keep trying right to the end in order to accomplish great things just like him.

This encounter with Mr Kiuchi had profoundly stimulated their awareness and thoughts – even captured their imaginations. This had raised their expectations of what they could achieve themselves in the future.

This experience led the teachers at Kuchiyokawa to make iterative changes both to the school's curriculum aims as well as to the scheme of work. The curriculum aims had been abstract and not personalised. This experience led teachers to adjust the school curriculum and scheme of work in order to capitalise on the way the Grade 5 students had found it powerful to use the opportunity of meeting Mr Kiuchi to focus specifically on their own futures.

The curriculum was reworded accordingly:

Before revision		After Revision
'Students meet community people who have particular life-roles as an opportunity to think about how to lead better lives as individuals'.	Lesson study ⟶ School curriculum revision	'Students meet community people who have particular life-roles as an opportunity to think about how better to lead their own lives'.

Further revisions were made to the curriculum in order that students in Grade 6 could deepen their learning in this dimension. The following year, the teachers carried out a lesson study designed to evaluate the extent to which a revised sequence of lessons for these same students could build upon and deepen the learning they had gained when they had met Mr Kiuchi in Grade 5. They wanted the pupils to think beyond their own lives and to learn how the kind of devotion and purposefulness they had witnessed from Mr Kiuchi might be broadened to a wider community perspective.

As a result they planned a series of research lessons based around a visit to the class from the curator of a nearby museum – The Museum of Nature and Human Activities in Hyogo. Like Mr Kiuchi the year before, the visit from the museum curator was planned as a stimulus to the unit which lasted 51 hours over a six-month period. His visit was intended to provide an opportunity for pupils to meet a person with a specialised field and to hear about his lifestyle from beyond their local community. They were encouraged to explore how the curator develops his insight into living things and the visit provided pupils with opportunities to explore how such people develop particular sets of ideas, beliefs and theories about their specialist field and its importance to others.

Conclusion

This has been an account of one school's development, revision and refinement of its integrated school curriculum and of how it used lesson studies systematically to evaluate the way that pupils learn that curriculum best and thus to develop better approaches to learning across the various curriculum dimensions encompassed by the integrated school curriculum. We can see that what results is a curriculum which not only helps children to develop knowledge, skills and understanding, but which does this in ways that reflect the school, its community and the values and character of the kind of people that the school wants its pupils to develop as adults.

This is made possible only by close, recursive study of how pupils are learning in the school curriculum and by refining and developing this learning and teaching as a continuous process not only of developing and teaching their pupils but equally as a continuous process of school curriculum renewal based upon its impact on the learning of the school's pupils.

I suggest here therefore, in addition to adopting LS as a means to improve learning and teaching in lessons, that practitioners and school and system leaders around the world should also pay attention to the potential that LS holds for development of the curriculum itself – a curriculum that is shaped around the minds of its learners and goals of its society (Matoba, 2012).

References

Aho, E., Pitkanen, K. and Sahlberg, P. (2006). *Policy and reform principles of basic and secondary education in Finland since 1968*. Washington, DC: World Bank, p. 14.

American Association of Colleges and Universities (2007). *College Learning for the New Global Century*. Washington, DC: AAC&U.

Ananiadou, K. and Claro, M. (2009). *21st Century Skills and Competences for New Millennium Learners in OECD Counties*. OECD Education Working Papers, no. 41. OECD Publishing.

Brown, J.S. and Duguid, P. (2002). Organising knowledge. In S. Little, P. Quintas and T. Ray (eds), *Managing Knowledge: an Essential Reader*. London: Sage.

Dede, C. (2007). *Transforming Education for 21st Century: New Pedagogies that Help All Students Attain Sophisticated Learning Outcomes*. Paper commissioned by the NCSU Friday Institute, North Carolina State University,

Raleigh, NC. Available: http://tdhahwiki.wikispaces.com/file/view/Dede_21stC-skills_semi-final.pdf

Dede, C. (2009). *Comparing Frameworks for '21st Century Skills'*. Unpublished paper. Cambridge, MA: Harvard Graduate School of Education, Harvard University. Available at: http://watertown.k12.ma.us/dept/ed_tech/research/pdf/ChrisDede.pdf

Desforges, C. (2012). *Re-designing the school curriculum for 2020: an opinion piece*. Nottingham: National College for School Leadership.

Dudley, P. (2013). Teacher learning in Lesson Study: What interaction-level discourse analysis revealed about how teachers utilised imagination, tacit knowledge of teaching and fresh evidence of pupils learning, to develop practice knowledge and so enhance their pupils' learning. *Teaching and Teacher Education*, 34: 107–21.

Hodgson, A. and Spours, K. (2003). The Learner Experience of Curriculum 2000: implications for the reform of 14–19 education in England. *Journal of Education Policy*, 20(1): 101–18.

Kuchiyokawa Kindergarten and Primary School (2003). *Research Bulletin: Development of Joint Curriculum between Kindergarten and Primary Education toward self-development ability of Children (Kenkyu Kiyou: Kodomo no jikoseicho-ryoku wo takameru Youji-kyouiku to Shougakkou-kyouiku no ittaiteki-kyouiku-katei no hennsei)*. Miki, Japan: Kuchiyokawa Kindergarten and Primary School.

Kuchiyokawa Kindergarten and Primary School (2005). *Research Report: Development of Joint Curriculum between Kindergarten and Primary Education toward Self-development Ability of Children – Focusing on 'Minagino-course' learning on development of way of life (Kenkyu Jissen Houkoku:Manabi no tanosisa afureru Youji-kyouiku to Shougakkou-kyouiku no ittaiteki-kyouiku-katei no hennsei Ikikata wo manabu Minagino Course wo kaku ni shite-)*. Miki, Japan: Kuchiyokawa Kindergarten and Primary School.

Kuno, H. (ed.) (2006). *'WAZA' for Lesson Designing Skills (Jugyo wo dezain suru 'waza')*. Tokyo: Gyousei.

Kuno, H. (2011). Conceptualizing Lesson Study as Change Management Recipe. In *Teacher Professional Development: Traditions and Changes*. Astana, Kazakhstan: Centre of Excellence, Nazarbayev Intellectual Schools, pp. 4–12.

Kuno, H. (2013). Forming and reforming the school-developed Curriculum through Lesson Study (Jugyo Kenkyu niyoru Gakkou Curriculum no Hensei to Kaitei). In M. Matoba and Y. Shibata (eds), *Lesson Study and Creation of Lessons (Jugyo Kenkyu to Jugyo no Sozo)*. Hiroshima: Keisui-sha, pp. 157–75.

Kuno, H. and Watanabe, S. (2009). New perspectives for development of Integrated Studies and Seikatu-ka under the concept of 'Knowledge-based society'. *Bulletin of Comprehensive Center for Education Practice*, vol. 12.

Kariya, Japan: Aichi University of Education, pp. 77–86. (http://hdl.handle.net/10424/1907)

Matoba, M. (2012). Lesson Study from world-wide perspectives – from WALS Tokyo conference in 2011 (Sekaino Jugyo Kenkyu, -Sekai Jugyo Kenkyu gakkai Tokyo Taikai yori-). Conference held by National Association for the Studies of Educational Methods (NASEM). *The Educational Methods (Kyoiku Houhou)*, 41: 142–54.

Mercer, N. (1995). *The Guided Construction of Knowledge: talk amongst teachers and learners*. Clevedon: Multiligngual Matters.

Metiri Group and NCREL (2003). *enGauge 21st Century Skills: Literacy in the Digital Age*. Chicago, IL: NCREL.

MEXT: Ministry of Education, Culture, Sports, Science and Technology (Monbu-Kagaku-sho) (2008). *Course of Studies, Teachers' handbook for Integrated Learning (Shougakkou Gakushu-Shido-Youryou Kaisetu, Sougoutekina-Gakushu-hen)*. Tokyo: Toyokan-Shuppan-sha.

Ministry of Education, Science and Culture (Monbu-sho) (1998). *Course of Studies (Shougakkou Gakushu-Shido-Youryou)*. Tokyo: Okura-sho-Insatsu-kyoku.

OECD (2011). *Building a High-Quality Teaching Profession: Lessons from Around the World*. OECD Publishing.

Partnership for 21st Century Skills (2006). *A State Leaders Action Guide to 21st Century Skills: A New Vision for Education*. Tucson, AZ: Partnership for 21st Century Skills.

Sato, M., Sawano, Y. and Kitamura, Y. (eds) (2009). *Changing the competency map in the world (Yureru Sekai no Gakuryoku map)*. Tokyo: Akashi-shoten.

Schleicher, A. (ed.) (2012). *Preparing Teachers and Developing School Leaders for the 21st Century: Lessons from around the World*. OECD Publishing.

Schön, D. (1983). *The Reflective Practitioner: How Professionals Think in Action*. New York: Basic Books.

Shulman, L. (1986). Those who understand knowledge growth in teaching. *Education Researcher*, 15(2): 4–14.

Wenger, E., McDermott, R.A., William, S. (2002). *Cultivating Communities of Practice: A Guide to Managing Knowledge*. Boston, MA: Harvard Business School Press.

Chapter 7

Prospects for further development of Lesson Study

David Pedder

In this brief endpiece I consider the simplicity of Lesson Study (LS) and the complexity of classrooms before going on to discuss three prospects for further developing the rich potential of LS for transforming the learning lives and relationships of teachers and students in classrooms, schools and networks.

The simplicity of Lesson Study and the complexity of classrooms

The chapters in this book report how LS can be a powerful means by which groups of teachers learn ways of further improving and adapting what they already do to support the learning of their students during classroom lessons and of creating new ways of supporting their student's classroom learning. Much of the simplicity and power of LS is discussed in relation to its proximity to the classroom environments in which teachers' professional learning and practice routinely develop. The clear classroom contextualisation of professional learning and practice development in LS contexts might explain why teachers are persuaded of its relevance to their work and their learning and practice needs.

And yet classrooms are complex and challenging places in which teaching and learning occur. The late and much lamented Donald McIntyre (2000) refers to the multidimensionality, simultaneity, unpredictability, publicness and historical embeddedness of the demands made on teachers in classroom lessons. In response to such complexity, he argues, teachers have learned to work effectively in classrooms through rigorous prioritisation, simplification and intuitive decision-making. By far the greatest part of the expertise which underpins how teachers think and support their students' learning effectively in classrooms is tacit, and necessarily so. Without such tacit processes teachers would quickly be overwhelmed by the constant flow of demands made on them. It is this understanding of the complexities of the classroom environment that has given rise to a traditional acceptance of teachers' classroom experience as private, isolated and therefore unshared; their expertise as mainly tacit, finding expression in what they do rather than in what they say; and their work, like their expertise, largely hidden from view behind the closed doors of their classrooms.

However, a number of innovations in classroom practice developed over the last 20 years or so have challenged this traditional portrayal of classrooms and how teachers develop their practice in them. Learning how to learn (James *et al.*, 2007), with its explicit and deliberate focus on how students learn and what practices students develop to enhance their learning and that of others is one example. Another is pupil consultation (Rudduck and McIntyre, 2007), with its explicit focus on how teachers teach and how teaching can be improved in light of students' suggestions for enhancing teachers' support for their (the students') learning. These are two examples of classroom innovations that can transform the tacit orders of classroom life and learning into more explicit and transparent encounters among learners – teachers and students alike. LS, with its deliberative and carefully staged cycles of highly detailed planning and evaluation, underpinned by explicit processes of exchange, creation and adaptation of knowledge and expertise is another similarly powerful innovation pushing through the tacit orders of traditionally conceived classroom life and challenging the portrayal of teachers living and working in a rather unsplendid isolation.

The arguments, and the beginnings of evidence for its success, have already been made clearly in the chapters of this book and need no repetition here. In this endpiece I would though like to consider three ideas for making LS even richer, more fruitful and more widely embedded in classrooms, schools and their networks.

I Going more deeply into learning

A key principle and purpose of LS is the improvement of learning. Learning – students' and teachers' – is the preeminent professional commitment of teachers. Teachers are routinely bound up in its promotion and practice, but not always critically so. LS fits very well with this routine preoccupation of teachers, and establishes learning as an explicit and visible focus of teachers' talk; and through such talk in planning and evaluation meetings, teachers can become more conscious of the how and why of learning as a means of enhancing ways they support their students in their learning. But in a LS group it is possible to refer to 'learning' repeatedly and uncritically without taking the risk of *going into* what members of a LS group mean by the term. One risk can be that the potential and richness of talk about 'learning' is pared down to a set of overriding purposes that define 'learning' in terms of narrowly construed outcomes and attainments. Learning outcomes and attainments are important. They can have important implications for students and their schools. However, to optimise the full potential of LS for enabling the richest possible learning experiences for both teachers and students, members of LS groups can critically reflect on whether or not the processes and procedures they adopt through particular cycles allow them to think through a wider range of understandings, perspectives and attitudes to learning and how these might inform their practice and collaborations in future LS cycles.

2 Students and teachers as partners in the Lesson Study process

Related to this is the scope and potential in the LS framework for building in opportunities for students to engage directly with their teachers in serious conversations about teaching, learning, curriculum and assessment. Such opportunities not only widen scope for teachers and pupils to develop and refine lessons together; pupils and teachers together would also be involved in the radical and essential work of making and re-making learning and relationships. LS, with its tight contextualisation in classroom lessons and clear collaborative procedures, provides a powerful framework for teachers not only to consult pupils about ideas to be included in a lesson or to elicit their evaluations about how a lesson that has already been taught might be further improved. Schools and teachers can also be encouraged to recognise their students as full partners in the process, and not just the academically high-performing students. This entails recognising students' maturity and capability of expressing insightful ideas about learning and elaborating helpful ways of supporting such learning in particular lessons. Pupil voice research (e.g., Rudduck and McIntyre, 2007) provides persuasive evidence that when schools and teachers recognise students as trustworthy partners, students articulate practically useful suggestions for improving the quality of learning, arrive at insightful evaluations of lessons and the rationales and ideas that underpin them, and adopt mature approaches to negotiating with their teachers practical ways of building new ideas into lessons.

The notion of students as partners involves a radical reconfiguration of the teacher–student relationship. It is always important to acknowledge that such reconfiguration of relationships and patterns of engagement are far from trivial and would further complicate teachers' already complex work. As with all significant pupil voice work that brings teachers and pupils into patterns of joint work and endeavour, teachers are challenged to change the way they see their role. So are their pupils. Pupils as well as teachers have an explicit role in planning and instigating classroom teaching and learning. Pupils are not merely cast as the objects of their teachers' practice but as co-constructors of their own effective teaching and learning processes, which is to say that both pupils and teachers have responsibility for teaching and learning.

The implications of this for school leadership are not trivial either. Schools need to be led as places in which learning is not reduced to a curriculum or testing package provided or delivered to a passive pupil by a teacher or a school or a government agency. Instead, using LS as a way of bringing teachers and pupils together as partners in learning and teaching, means that learning and teaching are shaped through negotiation, dialogue, conversation and consultation. Through such processes, students and teachers both become active agents of learning – their own and one another's. LS provides a simple but powerful and explicit set of arrangements and processes for fostering the dispositions, norms and practices of negotiation, dialogue, conversation and consultation that can underpin the partnership-based learning among teachers and students suggested here. What ensues is a field of pedagogic practice in which no one is free of the burdens of choice and decision-making. LS provides the practical means for freeing teachers from the requirement of shouldering burdens of choice and responsibility in isolation, not merely because LS brings teachers together, but because it provides a powerful context for a new pedagogic partnership with their pupils.

To understand LS, see its potential and then free up teachers to work together and commit to collaboration and trust-building in LS groups represents a challenging set of steps for any school leader. It takes a leader of particular courage and insight to then see the potential for replenishing pedagogic relationships in ways outlined above and then to commit resources and find ways of realising and embedding it in practice.

3 Networking Lesson Study

There are a growing number of clusters and networks of schools working with universities and agencies of education to promote LS at scale. The size and characteristics of these clusters and networks vary. The successful ones have either already developed or are working to develop infrastructures for supporting and promoting LS and for raising awareness and sharing knowledge about what has been learned and developed through LS with colleagues at other schools. The University of Leicester in the East Midlands region of the UK has been working closely with the Affinity Teaching School Alliance – a network of more than 60 primary schools in Leicestershire – since 2011 when Peter Dudley lead an inspiring workshop introducing LS to a hall full of primary teachers. Since then Affinity have grasped the nettle and have actively promoted LS as a major research-informed professional learning strategy throughout its network of schools. Affinity Teaching School Alliance and the University of Leicester have worked together to develop a knowledge production and sharing infrastructure to support the spread and uptake of LS and research-informed practice across a geographically dispersed group of primary schools. A cross-alliance partnership has formed between the University of Leicester, Affinity, the Leicester Teaching School Alliance and the Brooke Weston Teaching School Alliance (Northamptonshire) partly to build systems and opportunity for supporting teachers' use of LS and other kinds of research on a wider scale in the East Midlands region of the UK.

The knowledge-sharing infrastructure for supporting LS and other research at Affinity Teaching School Alliance (ATSA) can be summarised as follows:

a   Formulating and communicating ATSA strategic priorities for professional learning and practice development through LS and other kinds of research.

b   Supporting expansion in the quantity and quality of lesson studies and other research through Research and Innovation Champions at each school in ATSA – the Research Champions Network (RCN).

c   Supporting and coordinating the work of RCN through a Specialist Leader of Education in the role of ATSA's Research and Innovation network lead (SLE R+I Lead).

d   Providing guidance in translating teachers' practice-based challenges and problems into lesson studies and other research designs.

e   Evaluating research proposals into LS submitted by schools to the Research and Innovation Committee.

f   Commissioning small-scale teacher research through ATSA's research budget.

g   Supporting teachers to develop, use and adapt LS and critically consider the validity of claims developed through LS and other forms of research through workshops, methodological guidance and critical review.

h   Developing knowledge-sharing and dissemination forums and opportunities through ATSA's Online Learning Centre, regular research workshops, and annual cross-alliance research conferences with the University of Leicester, and Leicester and Brooke Weston TSAs.

The challenge for us at Affinity, Leicester and Brooke Weston TSAs and other networks and partnerships I have been involved in, is to support more and more teachers at more and more schools to develop awareness of and access to relevant research to inform development of their lesson studies, to realise their implications and relevance for further advancing the quality of classroom teaching, and to build research and LS into their normal patterns of professional work and practice.

Networking LS so that groups of schools can create local, situated knowledge shared within and across schools in ways that address schools' own priorities and agendas is a fruitful way forward and a great deal of networking activity reflects these more local purposes. Bringing networks together to work on a coordinated set of research projects, as is the case with the cross alliance partnership between Affinity, Leicester, and Brooke Weston TSAs and the University of Leicester, is one way of expanding this still fairly local model of networking and putting new practices to test and examination in a wider range of contexts than is possible when any particular school attempts to develop LS in isolation.

References

James, M., Black, P., Carmichael, P., Drummond, M-J., Fox, A., Honour, L., MacBeath, J., Marshall, B., McCormick, R., Pedder, D., Procter, R.,

Swaffield, S., Swann, J. and Wiliam, D. (2007). *Improving Learning How to Learn: Classrooms, Schools and Networks*. London: Routledge.

McIntyre, D. (2000). Has classroom teaching served its day? In B. Moon., M. Ben-Peretz and S. Brown (eds) *The Routledge International Companion to Education*. London: Routledge, pp. 83–108.

Rudduck, J. and McIntyre, D. (2007). *Improving Learning through Consulting Pupils*. London: Routledge.

Index

accountability 62, 65, 68, 75
across school systems 75–84
Action Education (AE) 35
action-learning sets 82
active listening 64–5
Adamson, B. 49
Affinity Teaching School Alliance 149
age phases 68, 71
Aho, E. 129
Alloway, T.P. 89, 93
appraisal 69
Australian Education Index (AUEI) 50

barriers to learning 88–90
benefits and constraints 38–45
Bransford, J. xvii
British Ability Scales (BASSII) 88
British Education Index (BEI) 50
Brooke Weston Teaching School
  Alliance 149

Caddington School 68–75
case pupils 7, 11, 69
case reports 98–100, 101, 103–4
challenges introducing LS 60, 61,
  62, 66
Chassels, C. 109, 116
China 13, 29
coasting schools 59
cognitive dissonance 12, 46
collaborative enquiry 60
Community of Practice 68, 115, 124
Competency Catalogue 135
complexity of classrooms 145
conditions and factors 46–7

constraints and challenges 44–7
contemporary learning
  theory xvii–xviii
continuing professional development
  (CPD) xv, xvii, 1, 45, 65, 71
contrived collegiality 49
cost 73, 83
Curriculum 2000 129

Davies, P. 111
Desforges, C. 1, 24, 129
Design Study 34
dialectic 16
direct instruction xvi
discovery learning xvi
Dudley, P. 46, 48, 59, 61, 111, 113,
  114, 115, 149
Dunnill, R. 111
dyslexia 89

Early Years 81, 82, 135
Economic and Social Research
  Council (ESRC) 33
Education Resources Information
  Center (ERIC) 50
expert see knowledgeable other
explicit focus on pupil learning 41
exploratory talk 19, 46

Farrell, T.S.C. 108
Fernandez, M.L. 111
Finland 129
'flexible people' 66
forensic examination 63
'front-load cover' 66

Fullan, Michael 67
funding 61

Galanouli, D. 111
Gathercole, S.E. 89, 93
global movement 22–4
Goal Attainment Scaling (GAS) 100
Goal Monitoring and Evaluation
    (GME) 100, 102
governors 67
group protocol 6–7

Hadfield, M. 15
Hattie, John 64
headteachers 77, 78, 80
Heibert, J. 29, 30, 34, 108
*Heisei 10 Japanese National
    Curriculum* 128, 130
*Heisei 20 Japanese National
    Curriculum* 128
hypothesising 12, 19, 21

Illeris, K. 124
improved quality 42–3
initial teacher education (ITE) 33, 36,
    45, 107–25; pedagogy in 120–2
Integrated Studies 130–2; developing
    a framework for 134; methodology
    137–8
intermental zone 16
*International Journal for Lesson and
    Learning Studies* 24
intersubjectivity 16
interthinking 16

Japan 13, 29, 128–42
Japanese approach 109, 116
Japanese schools 62
Japan International Cooperation
    Agency (JICA) 23
joint professional development
    (JPD) 5, 65
Jordan, Gill 15, 59, 76–9

Keli 35
Kelly, N. 89
Kiuchi, Tomoya 140

'knowledge is sticky' 67
knowledgeable others 75, 76, 80
Kuchiyokawa elementary school
    134–8, 139

Lang, Jean 15, 59, 75, 76, 79–84
Law, D.Y.K. 46, 109, 116
leadership of LS within and across
    groups of schools 75–6
leading LS 60–3
Leading Teachers 14, 76
learning 10, 146–7
learning community 133
learning environment 70, 72
Learning How to Learn Project 33
Learning moments 137, 138
learning points 19
Learning Study 24, 34
Leavy, A.M. 109
Leicester Teaching School
    Alliance 149
Leikin, R. 45
Lesson Study (LS): culture 63; cycle
    5, 8, 37, 62, 115, 116; definition 5,
    29; impact on school results 14; in
    initial teacher education 107–25;
    networking 149; prospects for
    further development 145–50;
    sharing knowledge and insights
    20; students and teachers as
    partners 147–8
Lesson Study for the Learning
    Community 34, 47
Lesson Study Handbook 114
Lesson Study-MLD (LS-MLD)
    project 86–105; case report data
    98–100; findings 90–104; impact
    on teachers 92–5; phases 87,
    92, 98, 99, 100; pupil outcomes
    100–2; research methods 90;
    teacher interviews 95–8
Lesson Study Research Group 41
Lewis, A. 89
Lewis, C. 14, 52
Lewis, C.C. 47
Lim, C. 32, 46
Lim, C.S. 36

literature search 50
London Schools Excellence Fund
　programme 14

master classes 83; *see also* 'open
　house', public research lessons
McIntyre, D. 145
McKinsey Reports 23, 63
Melville, W. 109, 116
mentors 107, 113, 114, 116, 117
Mercer, N. 46
methodology 51
micro-level observation 72
micro-level planning 16
micro-teaching 36, 112
Microteaching Lesson Study
　(MLS) 111, 112
MLD *see* Moderate Learning
　Difficulties
Moderate Learning Difficulties
　(MLD) 86; government
　definition 88

National Strategies 15
networking LS 149
non-contact time 66
Norwich, B. 89

observing learning 10
ofsted inspections 62, 81
'open house' 77, 83
Open House Lesson Study 34
organisational learning 71
organisational support 47
O'Shea, Jim 59, 61, 63–8
ownership 70

Pawson, R. 90
Peacock, Dame Alison 62
pedagogic black box 120–2
Pedagogical Content Knowledge
　(PCK) 12, 133
peer teaching 36
Pella, S. 46
performance management 62
Perry, R.R. 47
'plumbed in' 66, 67, 84

posters 78–9
post lesson discussion protocol 11
Primary National Strategies
　initiative 33
processes through which teachers
　learn 45–6
professional learning communities
　xviii, 38–40
Programme for International Student
　Assessment (PISA) 13
protocols 69; *see also* group protocol,
　post lesson discussion protocol
public research lessons 20, 34, 83
public teaching 13
Puchner, L.D. 38

questionnaire 91

Raising Levels of Achievement for
　Pupils with Moderate Learning
　Difficulties (Lesson Study-MLD
　project) 86; *see also* Lesson
　Study-MLD project
real classrooms xvi–xvii
Realist Evaluation 90
rehearsed lesson dialogue 21
'research base' 68
research findings: critical discussion
　48–9; focus and finding 37–47;
　growth and geographical spread
　31–2; sample characteristics 33;
　school settings and subject
　focus 32
research lessons 7; analysing 16–17;
　conducting 8; discussing and
　analysing 11; passing on learning
　13; planning 16–17
research programmes 14
Robinson, N. 45
Robinson, Vivienne 60
Rock, T.C. 110
role 17, 21

St Aloysius Junior School,
　Camden 63–8
Saito, E. 34, 47
samples 33

School-Centred Initial Teacher
    training (SCITT) 123
School Direct Training
    Programme 122
'See, Hear, Clear' 70
'Self' 70–1
SEN *see* special educational needs
sharing knowledge and insights 20
sharing learning 22
Shulman, L. 133
simplicity of LS 145
Sims, L. 109, 111
simulation 46
Singapore 47
situated learning theory 48
socio-cultural learning theory 16
special educational needs (SEN) 86
Special Educational Needs Code of
    Practice 88
staff cover 60 *see also* supply staff
standards in assessment 84
'sticky': knowledge 67; practice
    knowledge 133
Stigler, J.W. 29, 30, 34
supply staff 73; budget 66, 83

tacit knowledge 16, 21–2, 133
talk, teacher learning through 17
Taylor, A.R. 38
Teach for America 108
teacher collaboration 38–40
teacher knowledge, practice and
    professionalism 40
teacher learning 3, 4, 65; processes
    through which 45; tacit knowledge
    and 16; through talk 17
Teacher Learning Communities
    (TLCs) 67

Teach First 108, 122, 123
Teaching and Learning Research
    Programme (TLRP) 33
*Teaching Gap: Best Ideas from the
    World's Teachers for Improving
    Education in the Classroom* 29
teaching quality grades 62
Teague, Sue 59, 68–75
test results 84
Tilley, N. 90
time 61, 64, 74; non-contact 66
'transfer of training' issue xv
Trends in International Mathematics
    and Science Study (TIMSS) 13, 29
Tsui, A.B.M. 46, 109, 116

unconditional positive regard 6
unconscious interventions 15–16
unintended outcomes 61, 65
United States 13, 30, 133
University of Leicester 23, 149;
    evaluation 116–20; model 113–20

Variation Theory 34–5
variations and adaptations 34
videos 37, 78, 95
Vietnam 47
visible learning 64

Walker, E. 49
Walsh, D. 109, 111
web-based platforms 23
well-being, staff xix
White, A.L. 36
Wiliam, D. xviii, 66
working memory 89–90
World Association of Lesson Studies
    (WALS) 23, 31